Assignments in AutoCAD

Other titles from Bob McFarlane

Beginning AutoCAD ISBN 0 340 58571 4
Progressing with AutoCAD ISBN 0 340 60173 6
Introducing 3DAutoCAD ISBN 0 340 61456 0
Solid Modelling with AutoCAD ISBN 0 340 63204 6
Starting with AutoCAD LT ISBN 0 340 62543 0
Advancing with AutoCAD LT ISBN 0 340 64579 2
3D Draughting using AutoCAD ISBN 0 340 67782 1
Beginning AutoCAD R13 for Windows ISBN 0 340 64572 5
Advancing with AutoCAD R13 for Windows ISBN 0 340 69187 5
Modelling with AutoCAD R13 for Windows ISBN 0 340 69251 0

Assignments in AutoCAD

Robert McFarlane
Senior Lecturer, Department of Integrated Engineering, Motherwell College

A member of the Hodder Headline Group
LONDON • SYDNEY • AUCKLAND
Copublished in North, Central and South America by
John Wiley & Sons, Inc., New York • Toronto

Published in Great Britain in 1997 by
Arnold, a member of the Hodder Headline Group
338 Euston Road, London NW1 3BH

Copublished in North, Central and South America by
John Wiley & Sons, Inc., 605 Third Avenue,
New York, NY 10158-0012

British Library Cataloguing in Publication Data
A catalogue record for this book is available from the British Library

ISBN 0 340 69181 6
ISBN 0 470 244151 (Wiley)

Produced by Gray Publishing, Tunbridge Wells, Kent
Printed and bound in Great Britain by JW Arrowsmith Ltd, Bristol

Assignment list

Preface

This book is for the AutoCAD user who requires additional examples on which to practise draughting skills. There is no write-up to accompany the drawings, but hints are given on how some of the activities can be attempted. My aim with the book is to let readers work out how to complete each exercise on their own.

The book will be an invaluable aid to *all* AutoCAD users using R12, R13 and LT, as well as anyone still using pre-R12 releases. The assignments can also be completed using Release 14 and (hopefully) any future releases. It will provide useful back-up material for all students studying any SQA or City & Guild CAD courses.

As the majority of the activities will be completed on A3-sized paper, I would recommend that the following standard sheet (or prototype drawing) is made:

1. Name **STDA3**
2. Limits: from 0, 0 to 420, 297
3. Units: decimal to 2DP, angles to 1DP

4. Layers:	OUT	red	continuous
	CL	green	center
	HID	9	hidden
	DIM	magenta	continuous
	SECT	cyan	continuous
	TEXT	blue	continuous
	CONS	yellow	continuous
5. Text style:	name	STDA3	
	font	romans	
	value	accept all defaults (including 0 height)	
6. Dimension style:	name	STDA3	

Settings and values to suit individual/company requirements.

7. Grid: 10
   Snap: 5

8. Drawing area: a rectangle drawn on layer 0:
    (a) from 0, 0
    (b) to 380, 270.
9. All drawings should be saved:
    (a) in a named directory
    (b) on a floppy disk.

    It's your choice.

I hope that you enjoy completing the exercises in the book, and if you have any suggestions for other examples, I would be more than happy to hear from you.

Good luck

Bob McFarlane

Acknowledgements

This book would not have been possible without the inspiration given to me by the work of other AutoCAD authors. I must admit that I find it extremely difficult to think up original ideas for CAD, and for this reason I must thank the following authors for allowing me to use their ideas:

Tim McCarthy	*AutoCAD Express*	Springer-Verlag
Brian Mayock	*Introduction to CAD*	Hodder
Bertoline	*AutoCAD for Engineering Graphics*	Macmillan/McGraw-Hill
Dr G. C. Lin	*Learning AutoCAD by Example*. Assignments 13, 48, 60	Reprinted with permission of Prentice Hall of Australia Pty Ltd

To all other AutoCAD authors, whose work is most appreciated.

Assignment 1

Simple shapes

Eight simple shapes to get you started.

1. (a) Grid on and set to 10
   (b) Snap on and set to 5.
2. Sizes are not important – use your imagination.
3. Commands used:
   LINE
   CIRCLE
   ARC: CSE method?
   DONUT
   ELLIPSE
   ERASE?
   REDRAW
4. Save as ASS_1.

Assignment 2

Three designs

The three designs are interesting to complete.

A. Rectangle size is 200 × 140 and is divided into four equal rectangles.
Grid and snap set to 10.
LINE and DONUT only.

B. Construct a 90 sided square.
Set the grid and snap to 10.
Draw lines first then use the SOLID command.

C. Large circle diameter is 120 and the rest is your own.
Use CIRCLE, DONUT, ARC.

A
B
C

Assignment 3

Polyline shapes

Shapes which have all to be created from polylines, with a grid setting of 10 and a snap setting of 5.

A. Two simple arrowheads of varying width.

B. A polyline with varying length and width. I used widths of: 0, 2, 4, 6, 8, 10, 15 and 20.

C. A polyline arc 'snake' with a constant width of 5.

D. The largest square is a 70 sided polyline with width 2. The smaller squares are offset 'inwards' by 5.

E. Simple polyline arc drawn through 90 degrees with width 5. The arrowhead width varies from 15 to 0 with a length of 40.

F. Direction sign drawn from two polylines.

G. A polyline arc 'spiral' drawn with varying width. I used widths of 0, 2, 4, 6, 8 and 10. Each arc segment is drawn through 180 degrees.

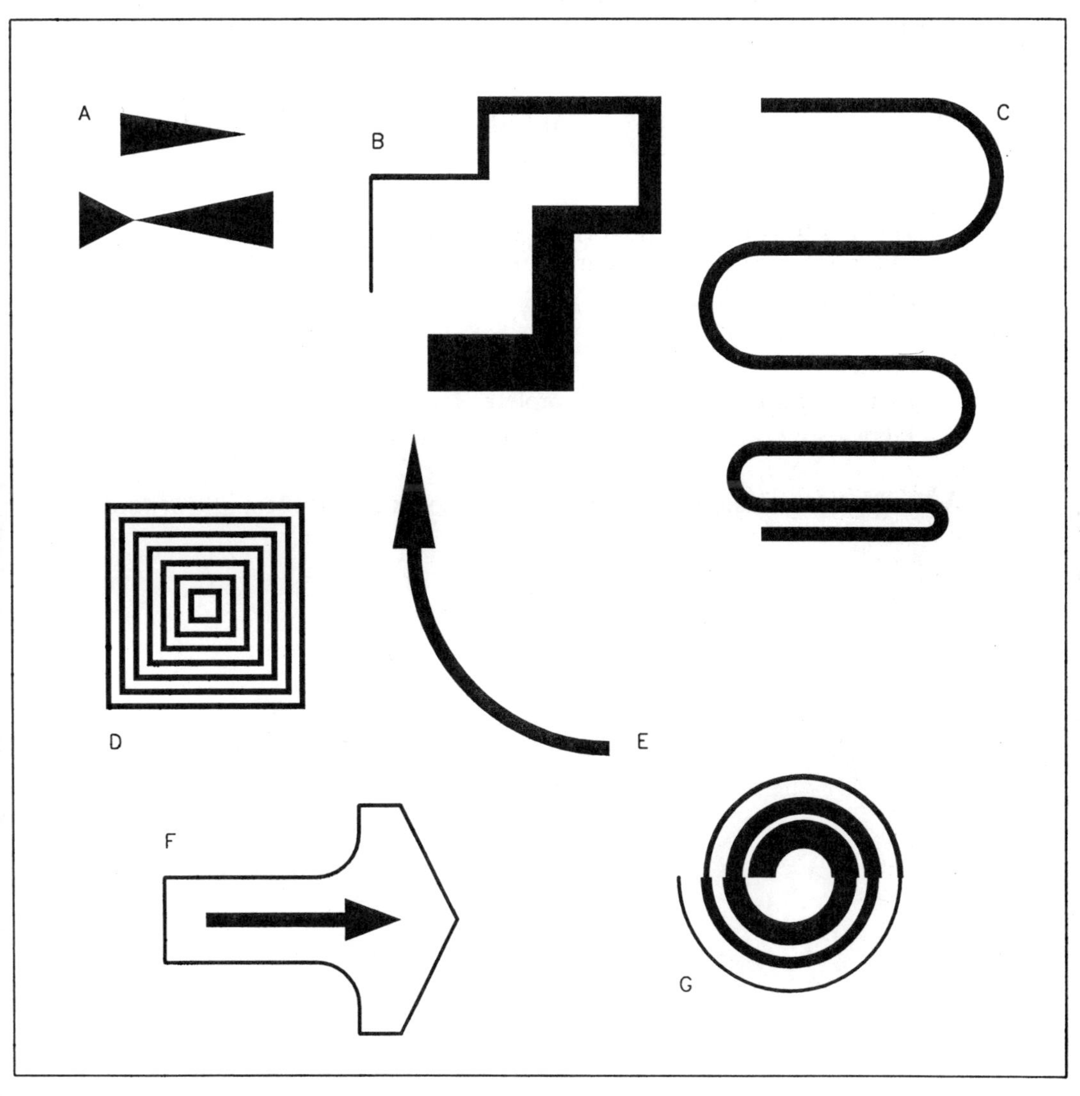
A
B
C
D
E
F
G

Assignment 4

Two components

The components have to be drawn with text and dimensions added.

1. *Hinge plate*
   Fairly simple to draw. Start at A (60, 100)
   Offset/change the hole centre lines?
   I set the LTSCALE to 12.

2. *Locator*
   Again a simple drawing to complete. The start point is B (260, 40)
   Draw using (a) relative/polar coordinate input or (b) offset and trim?

Adding the dimensions to the two components is fairly straightforward.

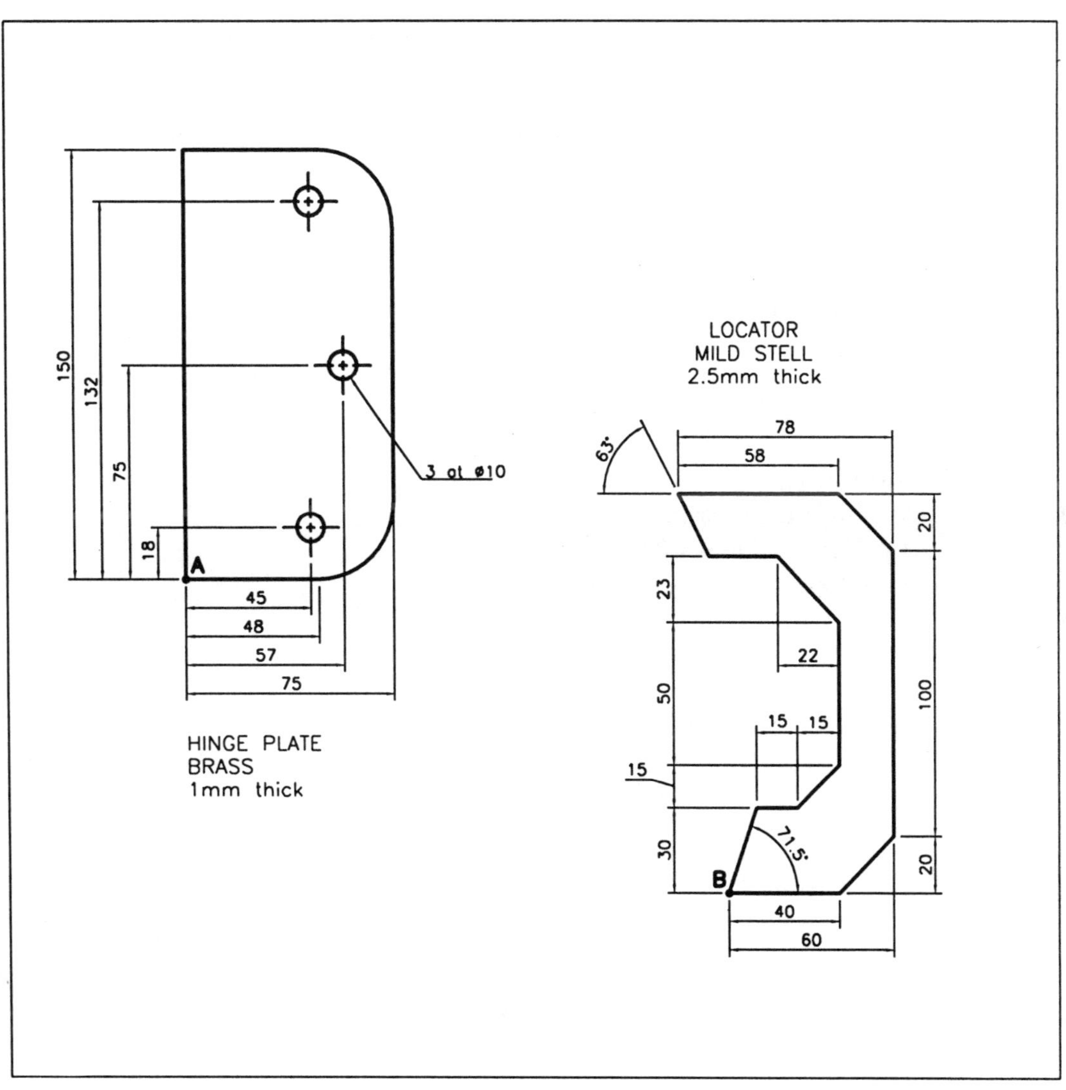
150
132
75
18
A
45
48
57
75
3 at ø10
HINGE PLATE
BRASS
1mm thick
LOCATOR
MILD STELL
2.5mm thick
63°
78
58
20
23
22
50
100
15 15
15
71.5°
30
B
20
40
60

Assignment 5

Another two components

Text and dimensions have to be added to each completed component.

1. *Rocker arm*
   An interesting drawing to complete and requires some knowledge of tangency.
   (a) Position the two circles first.
   (b) Add the 'straight line' parts next.
   (c) Add the arc entities as trimmed circles?
   (d) The dimensioning is straightforward.

2. *Stereo front*
   A simple drawing to complete.
   (a) The outline is a 0.8 width polyline.
   (b) The panels can be polylines or solids?
   (c) The design can be your own.
   (d) Baseline dimensions.

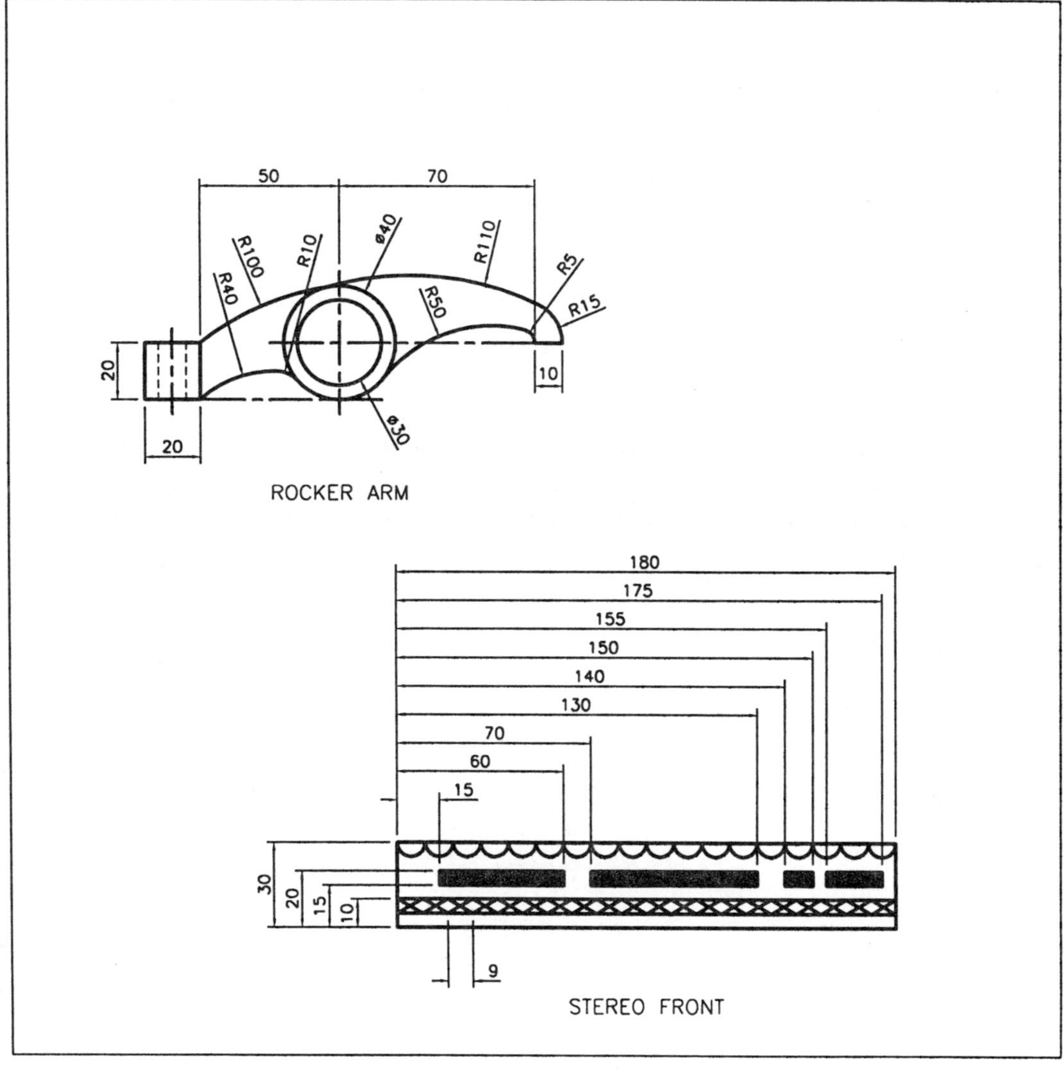
50
70
R100
R10
ø40
R110
R40
R5
R50
R15
20
10
ø30
20
ROCKER ARM
180
175
155
150
140
130
70
60
15
30
20
15
10
9
STEREO FRONT

Assignment 6

Car wheel designs

For obvious reasons this assignment is called 'car wheel designs'. The largest circle has a diameter of 110. I've tried to vary the designs as much as possible, but you can probably come up with better ideas.

1. Circles only, drawn in any position.
2. Circles and donut. Trimmed circle or arc? Polar array of course?
3. Harder than it looks. I used polar array.
4. An easy one.
5. Inscribed pentagon is the 'centre' of this design. The 'finger' effect takes some thought. I used a polyline/arc segment which had four different sized fingers then polar arrayed. Probably the hardest of the six.
6. This is harder than it would appear.

1
2
3
4
5
6

Assignment 7

Three components with dimensions

Three traditional type of components which have to be drawn with all dimensions added.

1. *Spacer 1*
   Fairly easy component using polar array.

2. *Hook*
   A nice tricky little problem for you, especially with the sizes given.
   Use the two centre lines as datums and offset as much as possible.
   Arcs are trimmed circles once their centres are positioned.
   The lines between the arcs are tan/tan lines.
   The dimensions require some thought.

3. *Spacer 2*
   No real problem once you position the circles. Offset and trim are useful. I created the slotted holes from trimmed circles and polar arrayed lines.
   The dimensions are easy!

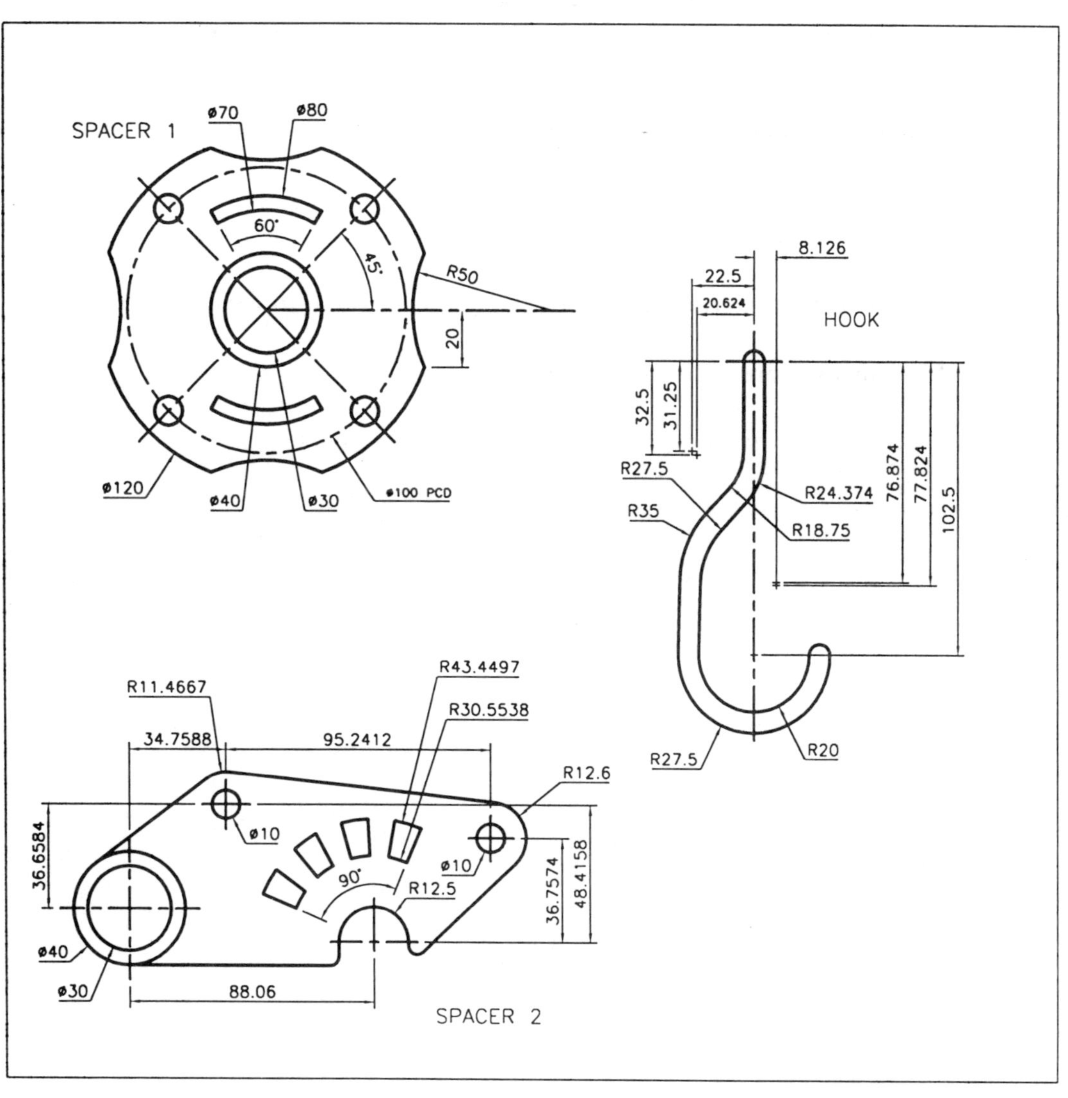

SPACER 1
ø70
ø80
60°
45°
R50
20
ø120
ø40
ø30
ø100 PCD
HOOK
8.126
22.5
20.624
32.5
31.25
R27.5
R35
R24.374
R18.75
76.874
77.824
102.5
R27.5
R20
R11.4667
R43.4497
R30.5538
34.7588
95.2412
R12.6
36.6584
ø10
ø10
90°
R12.5
36.7574
48.4158
ø40
ø30
88.06
SPACER 2

Assignment 8

Variation on a cube

Our first isometric drawing and it is very easy.

There are 12 'cubes' to be drawn. The basic cube size is 40 and the 'side' thickness is 10.

Set the isometric grid and snap to 10, and work with isoplane top active.

How many more such 'cubes' can be drawn?

Assignment 9

Isometric 1

A bracket drawing requiring two views and an isometric.

The two views are simple, hatching being added – I used BHATCH.

The isometric is interesting as it requires the trim command to be used quite a bit.

Remember that for 'circles' in isometric:

(a) set the correct isoplane
(b) R12 uses **iso** from the ELLIPSE command
(c) R13 requires ELLIPSE to be entered from the keyboard, then select the **I** option.

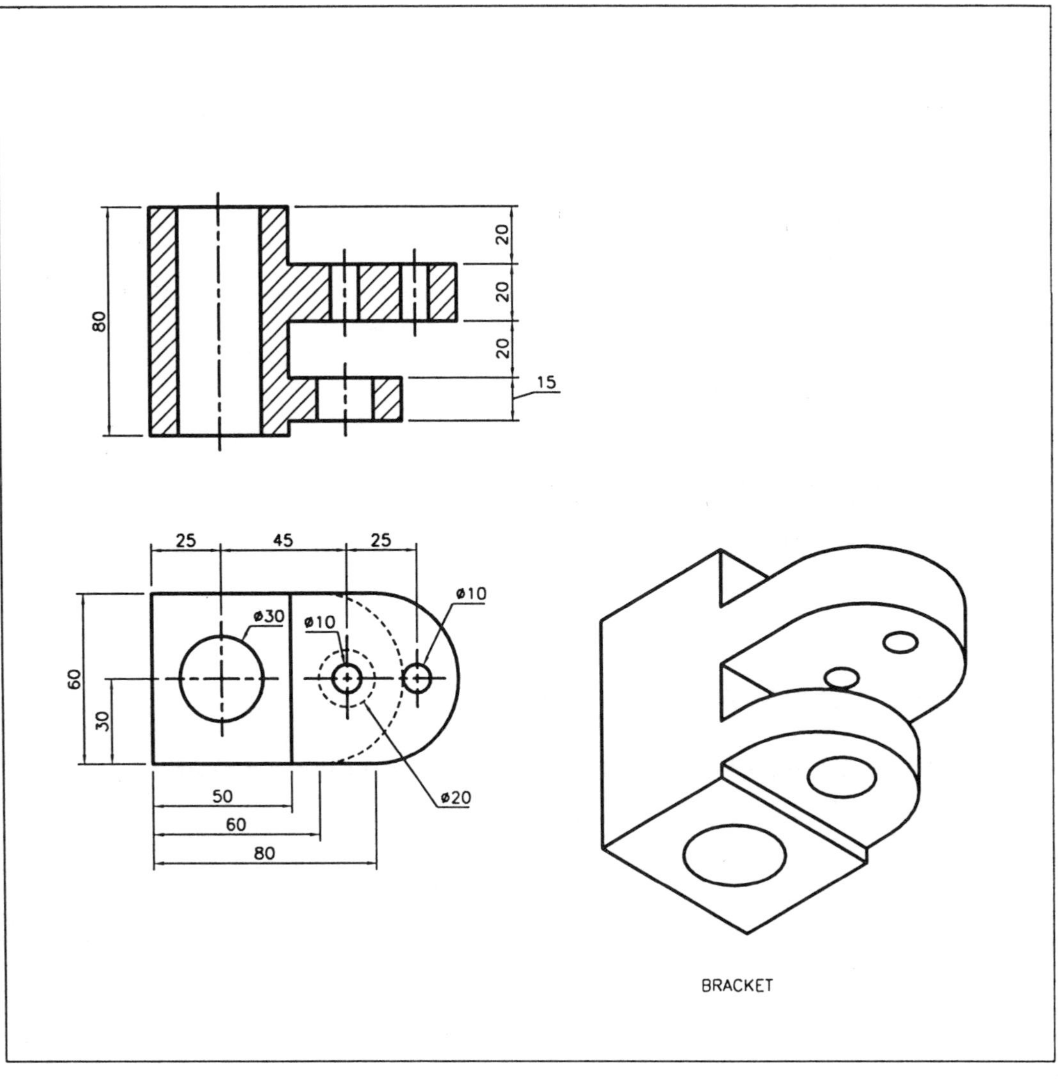

BRACKET

Assignment 10

Piping drawing

This is a scale drawing and has to be fully dimensioned with all text added. It requires the MVSETUP command to be used with the following entries:

(a) answer N to the enable paper space prompt
(b) units: metric
(c) scale: 15, i.e. 1:15
(d) A3 paper size, i.e. 420 width and 297 height.

Other parameters to be set are:

1. Grid: 150.
2. Snap: 75.
3. DIMSCALE: 15.
4. LTSCALE: 180.

The drawing can be completed by several different methods, but think about OFFSET, TRIM and CHANGE?

Adding the dimensions is simple, but think about the text height.

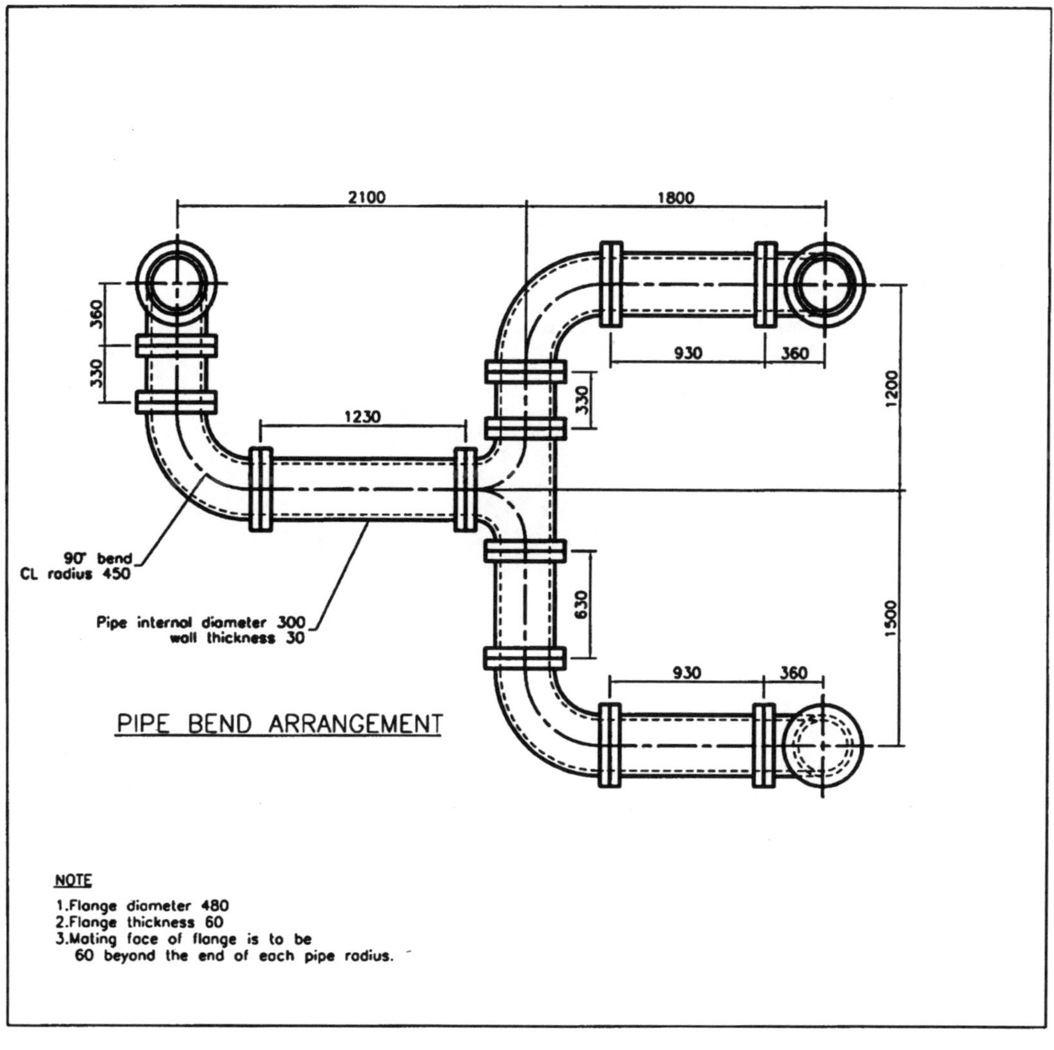
2100
1800
360
330
930
360
1200
1230
330
90° bend
CL radius 450
Pipe internal diameter 300
wall thickness 30
630
1500
930
360
PIPE BEND ARRANGEMENT
NOTE
1.Flange diameter 480
2.Flange thickness 60
3.Mating face of flange is to be
60 beyond the end of each pipe radius.

Assignment 11

Square deals

The two 'designs' start as squares.

A. Draw a square with 140 side.
   Offset 20 horizontally and vertically.
   Trim to give the final design.

B. Draw a 20 side square (snap on helps).
   Offset horizontally by 20.
   Multiple copy with snap on.
   Add a 5 wide closed polyline to complete the design.

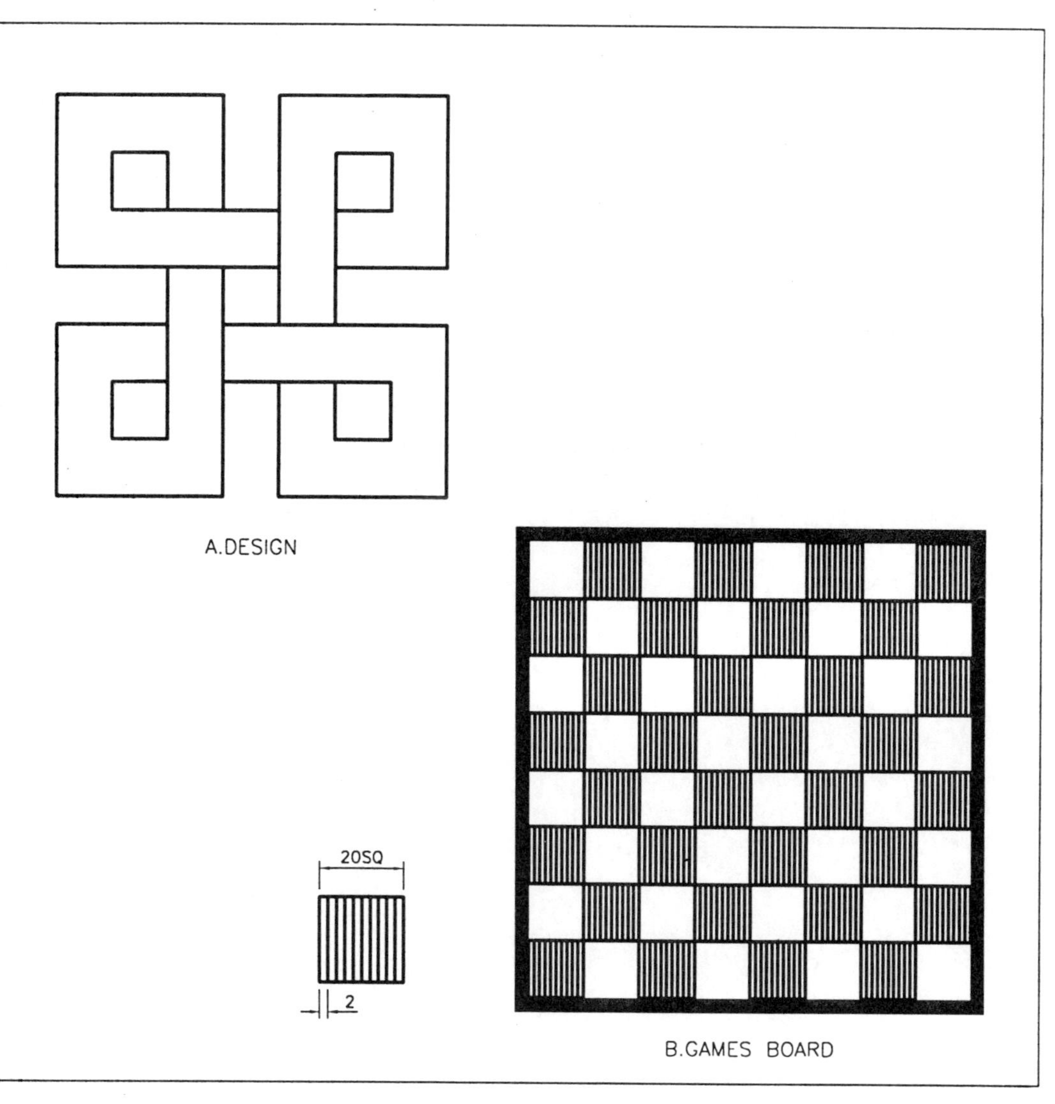

A.DESIGN

B.GAMES BOARD

Assignment 12

Tile patterns

The two tile patterns can be completed using multiple copy or rectangular array. I used array.

A. The square is 160 side.

B. The circle radius is 95.
Trim and erase need to be used.

If you use the array command you will need to work out the number of rows and columns, as well as the row and column distances.

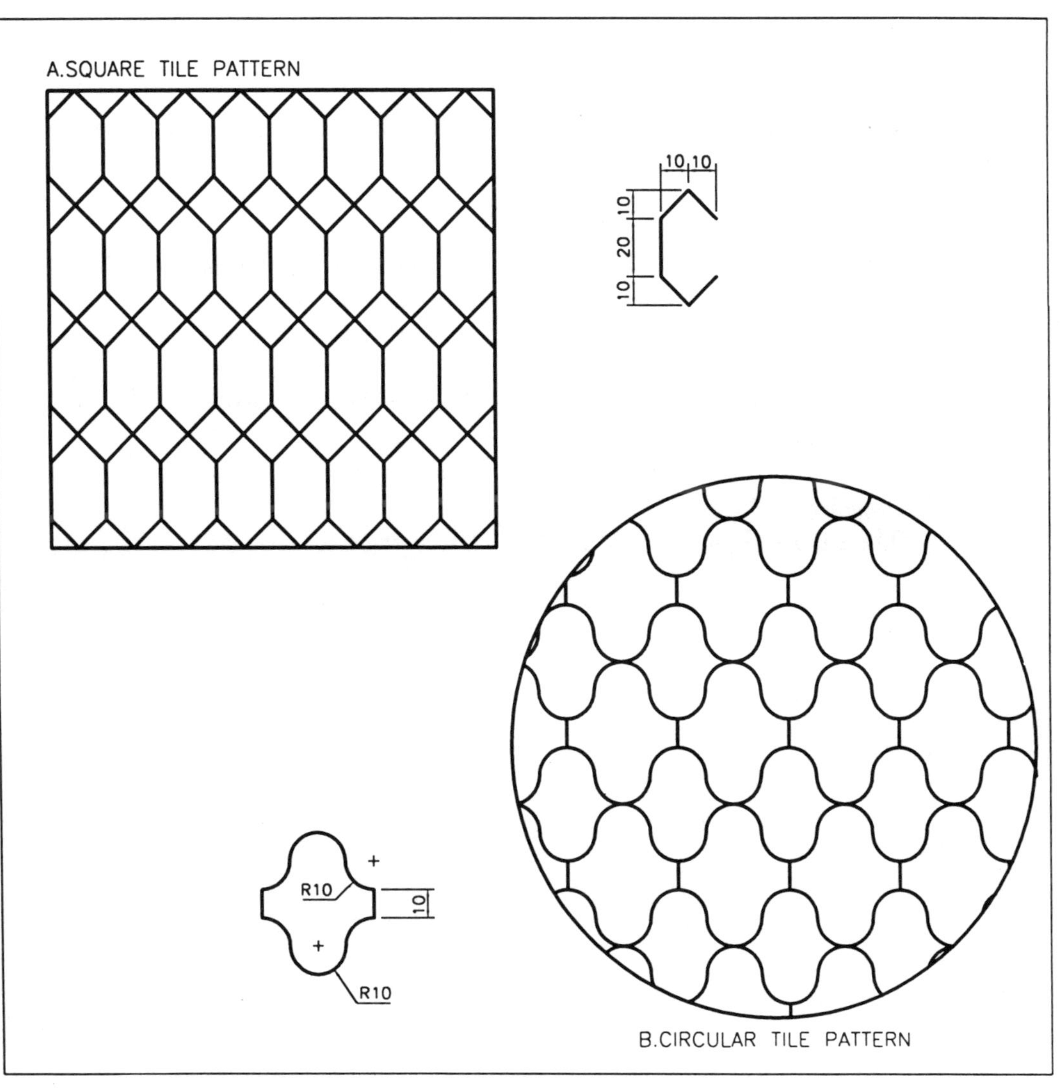
A.SQUARE TILE PATTERN
10
10
10
20
10
R10
R10
10
B.CIRCULAR TILE PATTERN

Assignment 13

Arrayed designs

Three different designs which all use the same basic star shape. The smaller shape has a scale factor of 0.5.

A. *Rectangular*
   Simple to construct, the only problem being the distances?
   The smaller star is 'centred' between the larger stars.

B. *Polar*
   Uses the same polar array centre point which can really be picked anywhere.

C. *Angular*
   The snapangle must be altered. My value was 10.

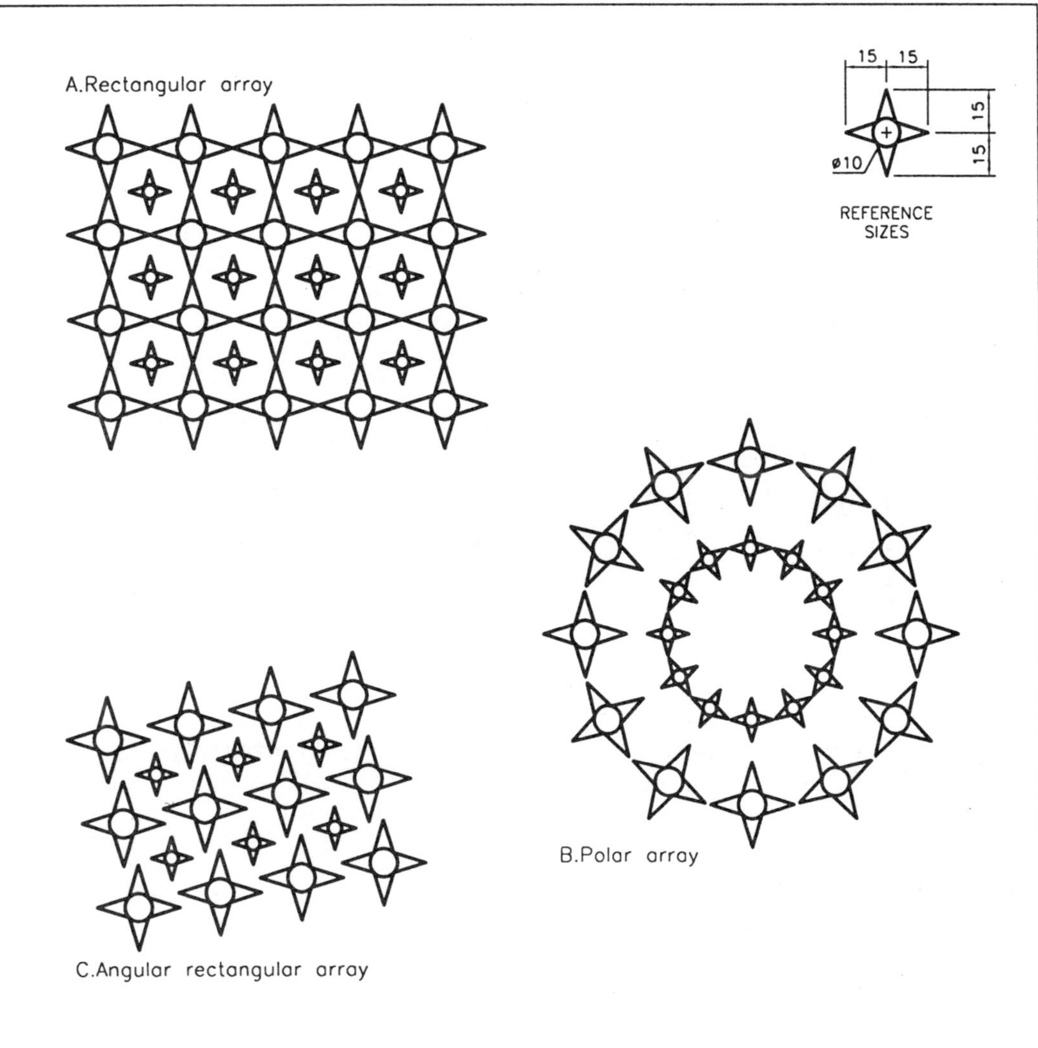
A.Rectangular array
15
15
15
15
ø10
REFERENCE
SIZES
B.Polar array
C.Angular rectangular array

Assignment 14

Oil platform

This exercise requires a knowledge of:

(a) the elevation and thickness commands
(b) paper space viewports
(c) the viewpoint command.

My recommendations are:

1. Set a two-viewport (vertical) configuration.
2. Use elevation and thickness to 'set' each of the five different levels from the following information:

Level	*Size*	*Height*	*Colour*
Legs	10 dia	80	red (arrayed?)
Base	90 dia	60	blue
Living	40 square	40	green
Store	pentagon inscribed dia 30	50	magenta
Tower	hexagon inscribed dia 20	70	cyan

3. Set two viewpoints:
   (a) from above
   (b) from below.
4. Hide and shade.

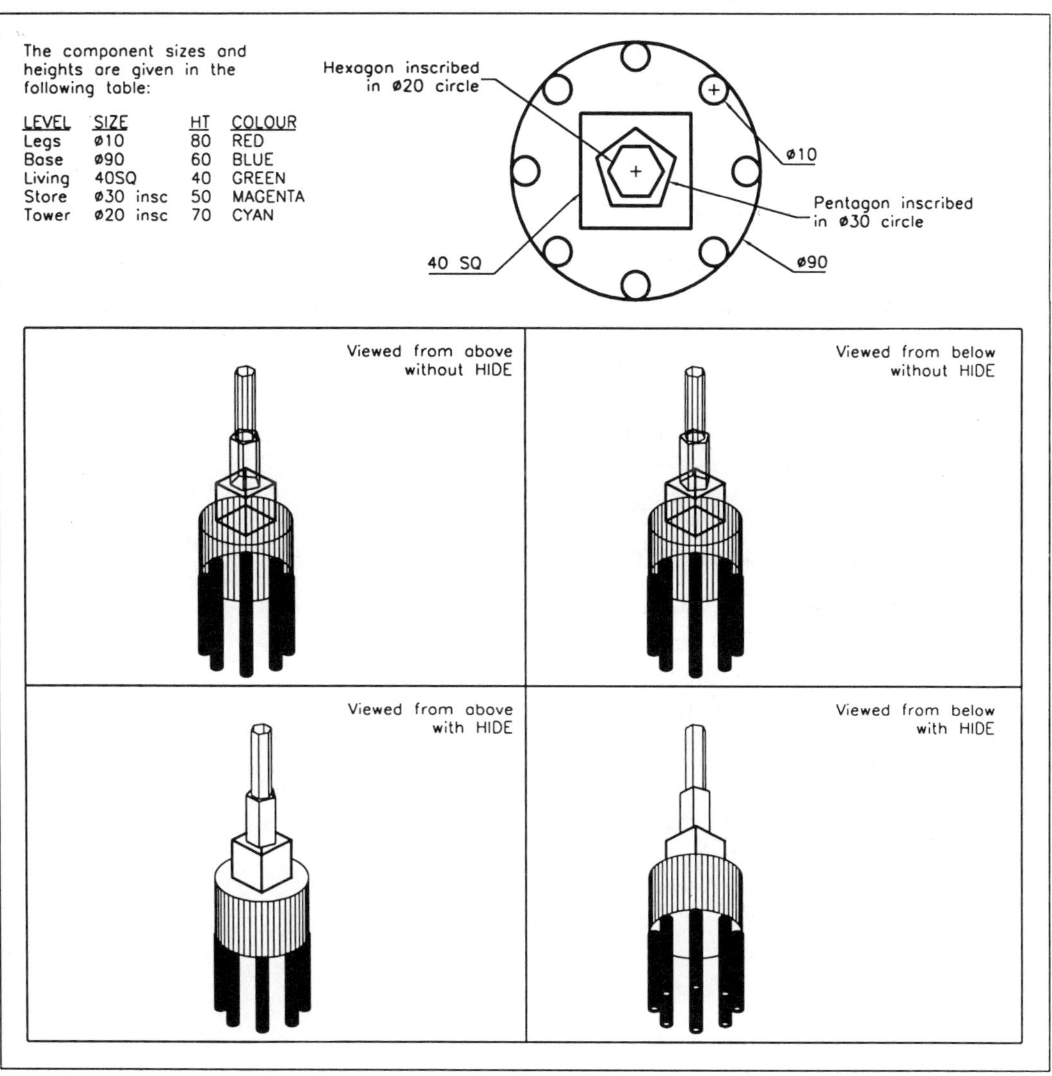
The component sizes and
heights are given in the
following table:
LEVEL SIZE HT COLOUR
Legs ø10 80 RED
Base ø90 60 BLUE
Living 40SQ 40 GREEN
Store ø30 insc 50 MAGENTA
Tower ø20 insc 70 CYAN
Hexagon inscribed
in ø20 circle
ø10
Pentagon inscribed
in ø30 circle
40 SQ
ø90
Viewed from above
without HIDE
Viewed from below
without HIDE
Viewed from above
with HIDE
Viewed from below
with HIDE

Assignment 15

Arc spiral

This design is created from arcs. The construction is as follows:

1. Set the snap to 3.
2. Draw a 3 mm square.
3. Zoom in on an area around this square.
4. Extend construction lines from the corners of the square as shown.
5. Draw an arc quadrant using the Centre–Start–Angle (CSA) method with:
   (a) point C1 as the centre point
   (b) point 1 as the start point
   (c) enter –90 as the angle.
6. Offset this arc by 3 'outwards'.
7. Repeat the CSA arc command with:
   (a) point C2 as the centre
   (b) point 2 as the start
   (c) enter –90 as the angle.
8. Offset this arc by 3 outwards.
9. Repeat the CSA again with:
   (a) centre at C3
   (b) start at 3
   (c) angle –90.
10. Offset by 3.
11. Zoom out.
12. Repeat the CSA and offset commands using the above steps as a guide. You work your way around the square taking each corner as the arc centre in turn, and the end of the previous arc as the start point. The angle is always –90 and the offset is always 3. You may want to zoom in on certain parts of the spiral.

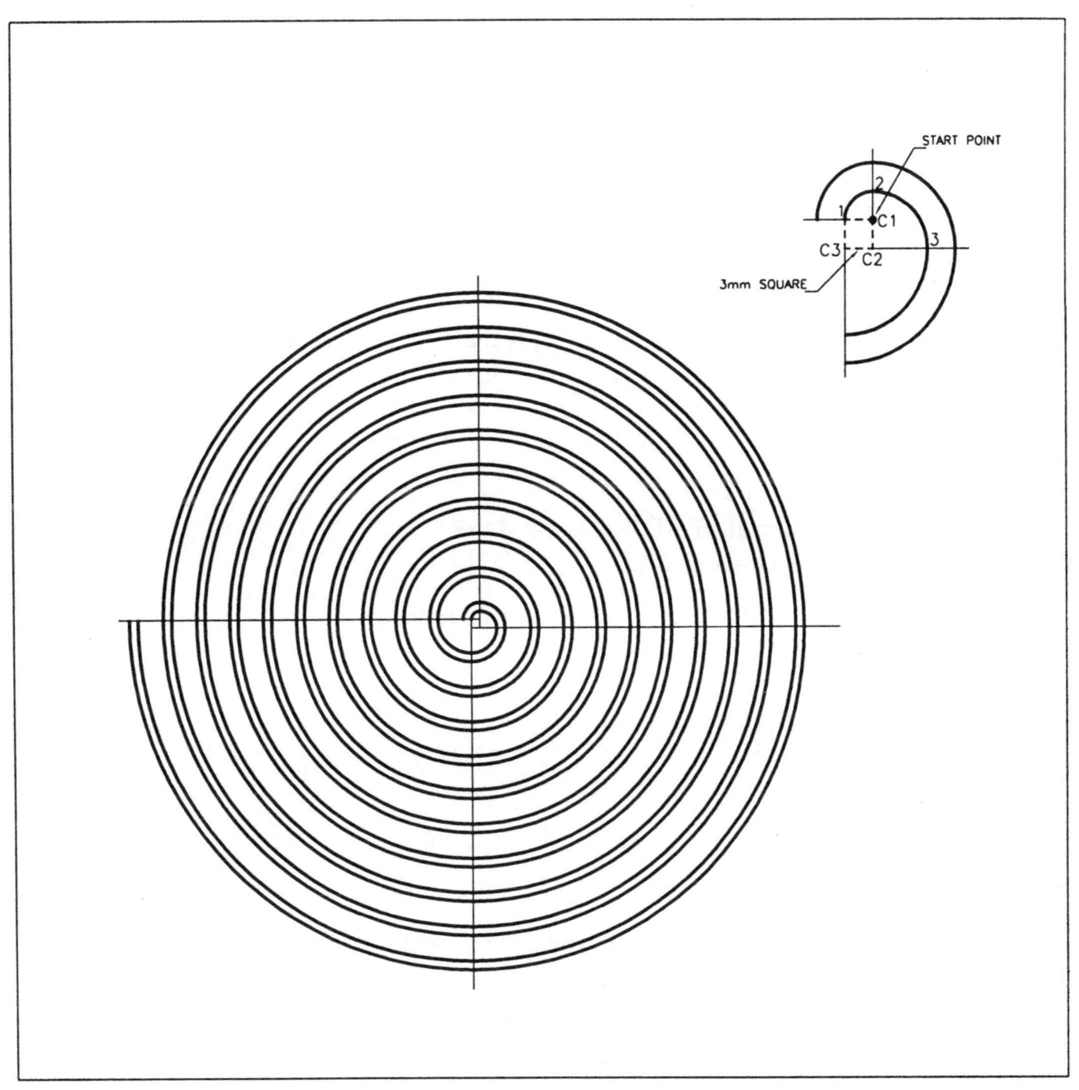
START POINT
2
1
C1
3
C3
C2
3mm SQUARE

Assignment 16

Component for dimensioning

The component has to be drawn with all dimensions and text added. The problem is that the drawing paper is set to an imperial size and requires several of the dimension variables to be altered.

1. Open your standard sheet and erase all borders.
2. Set the **LIMITS** to 0, 0 and 10, 8 then ZOOM-ALL.
3. Set the following variables:
   grid: 0.20
   snap: 0.1
   LTSCALE: 0.3
   Units: decimal to 4 DP
   Angles: decimal to 0 DP
4. Enter the following dimension variable values:
   dimtxt: 0.1
   dimasz: 0.15
   dimexo: 0.125
   dimexe: 0.15
   dimdli: 0.3
   dimcen: 0.05
   dimtvp: 0.1
   dimgap: 0.1
5. Draw and fully dimension the component.
   Note: (1) While I have set the dimvars from the keyboard, you can alter them from within the Dimension Styles. It is your choice.
   (2) You may want to alter other dimvars.
6. The text is to be added as shown, but at what height?

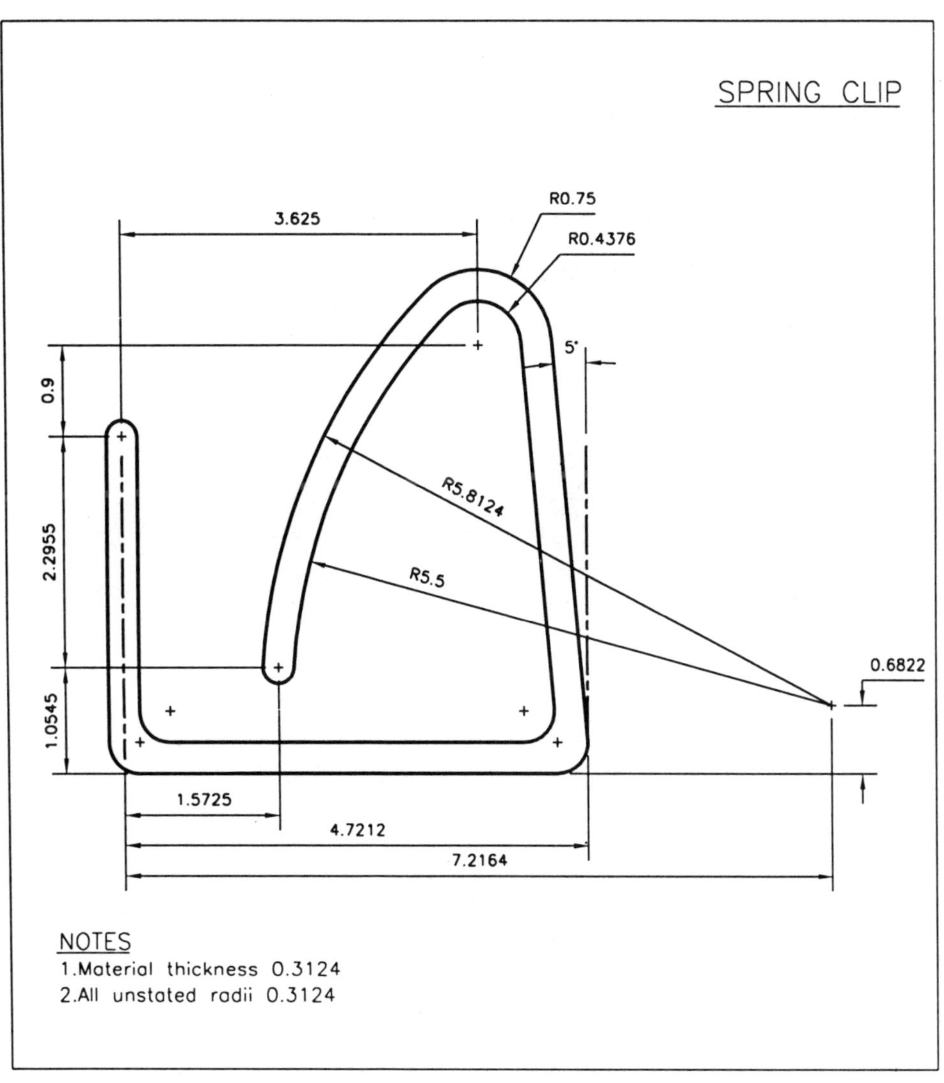
SPRING CLIP
3.625
R0.75
R0.4376
5°
0.9
2.2955
1.0545
R5.8124
R5.5
0.6822
1.5725
4.7212
7.2164
NOTES
1.Material thickness 0.3124
2.All unstated radii 0.3124

Assignment 17

Tangency

Five problems of varying difficulty.

Position as many centre lines and full circles as possible.

Arcs drawn as trimmed circles or fillets?

Add all dimensions as an additional exercise.

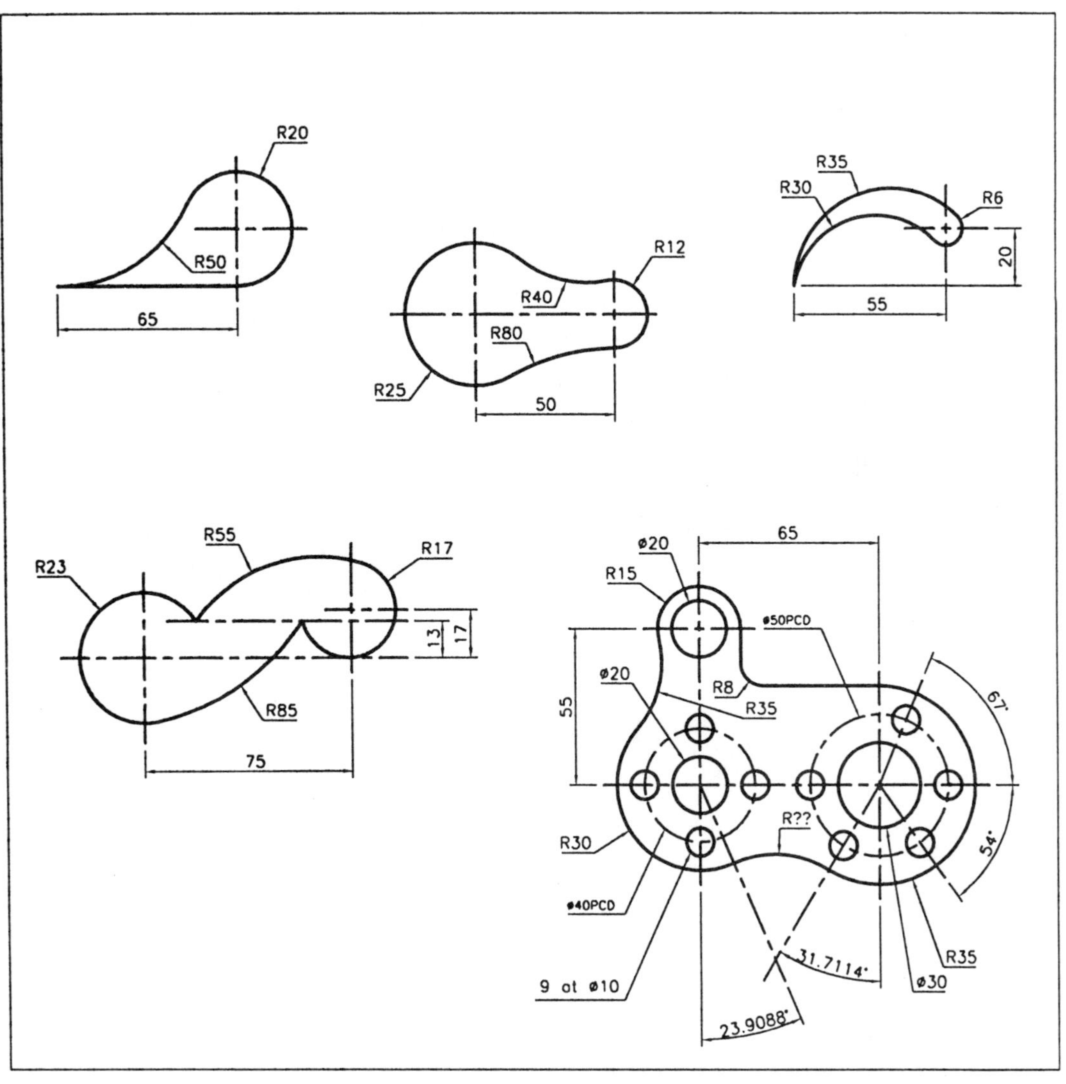
R20
R50
65
R12
R40
R80
R25
50
R35
R30
R6
20
55
R55
R17
R23
13
17
R85
75
ø20
65
R15
ø50PCD
ø20
R8
R35
67°
55
R30
R??
54°
ø40PCD
R35
31.7114°
ø30
9 at ø10
23.9088°

Assignment 18

Isometric cube design

1. Set the isometric grid to 10 and snap to 5.
2. Draw a 50 sided cube on the OUT layer.
3. Add isocircles to the three faces of the cube:
   (a) large radius 25, colour blue
   (b) small radius 15, colour green
   (c) toggle effect with CTRL E.
4. Using the arc CSE option, add three arcs between the isocircles then erase the original cube.
5. Scale the component by 0.5.
6. Produce the design pattern given.

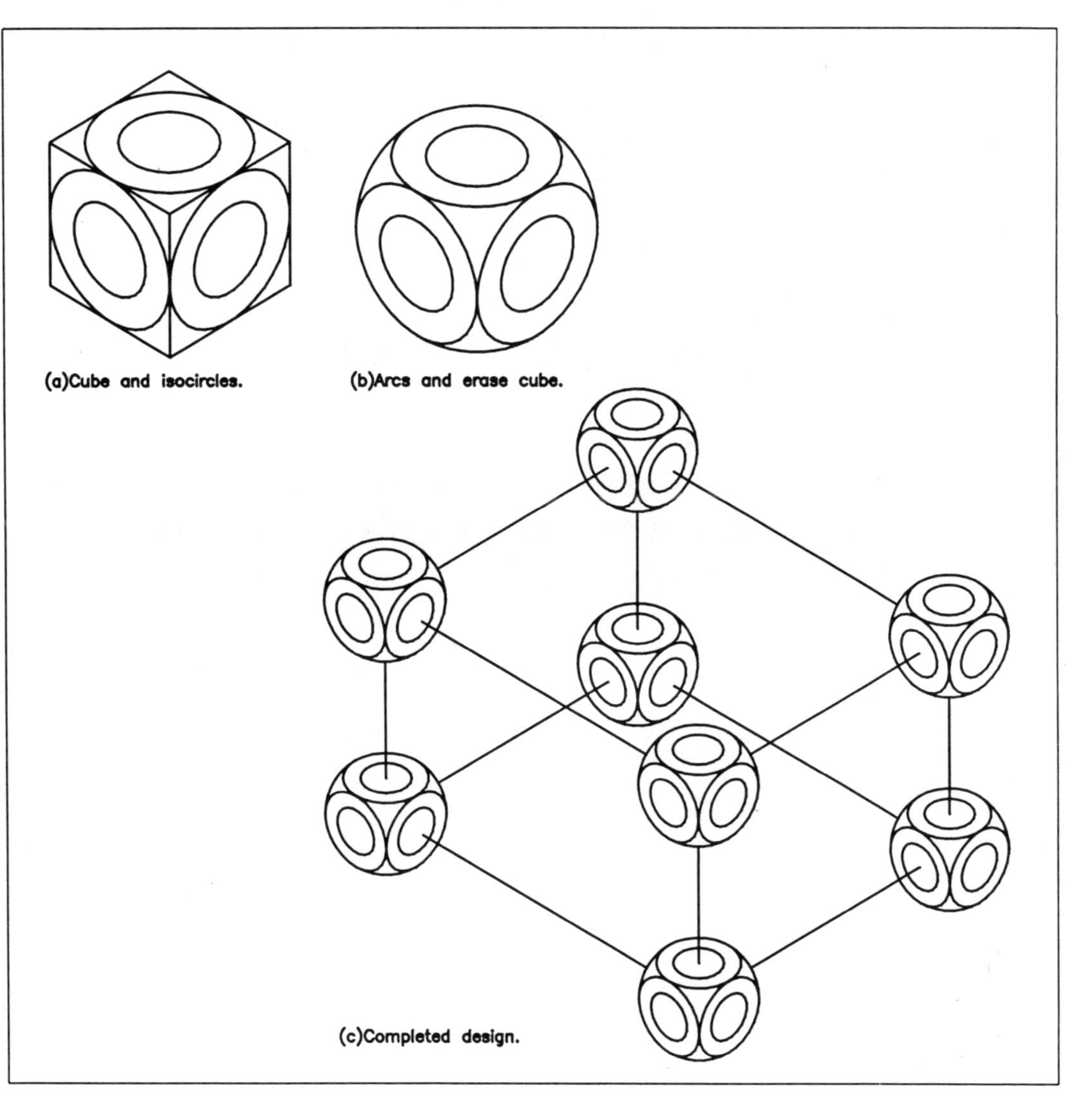
(a)Cube and isocircles.
(b)Arcs and erase cube.
(c)Completed design.

Assignment 19

Seeing is believing

The steps in the creation of the sunglasses are:

1. Select a suitable start point (snap on) and draw four lines as fig. (a) using relative polar coordinates:

from	start point
to	@63<283
to	@58<7
to	@63<98
to	@62<193
to	right-click

2. Fillet the four corners using the radii given in fig. (b).
3. Complete one side of the sunglasses using the information in fig. (c).
4. Mirror to complete the model.

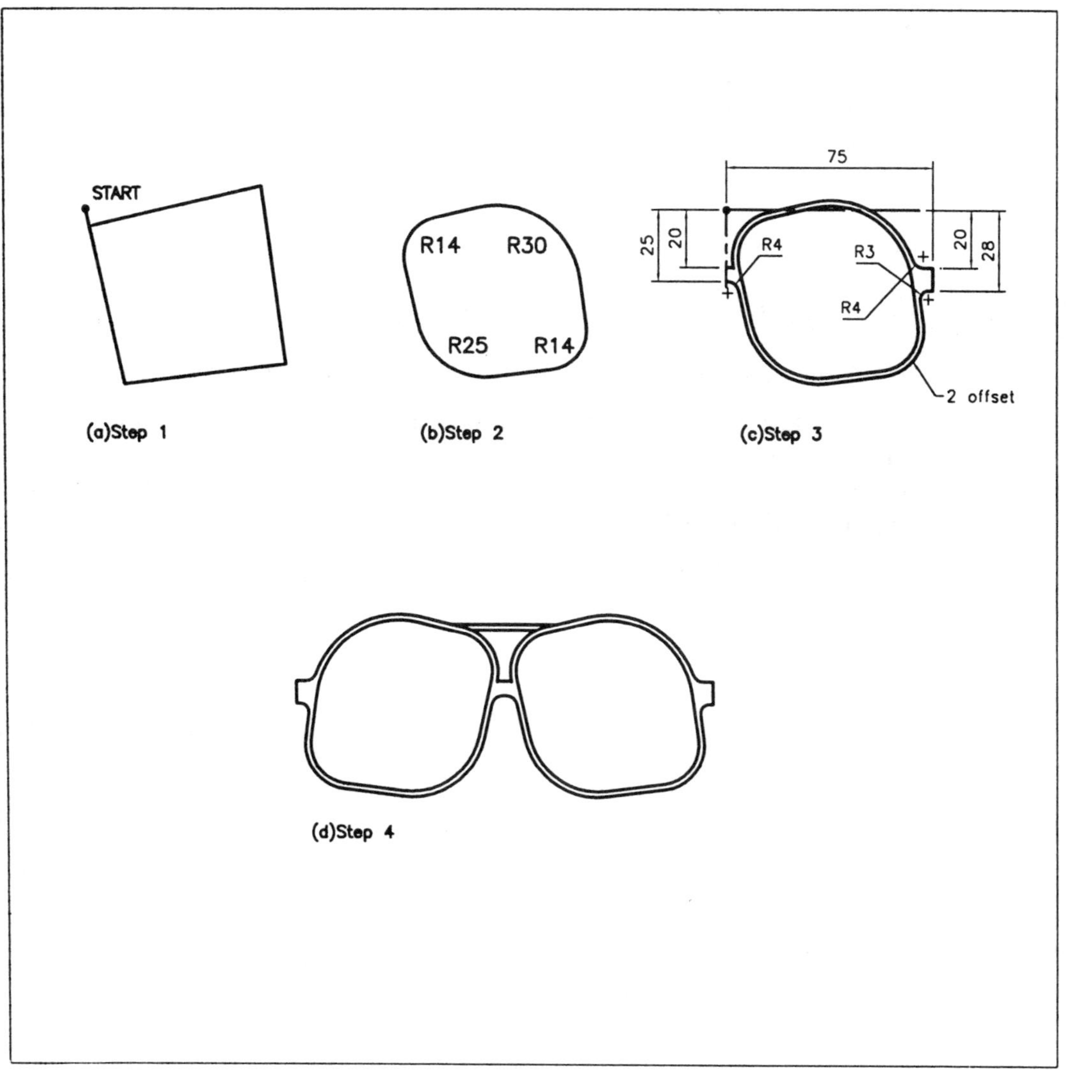

(a)Step 1
(b)Step 2
(c)Step 3
(d)Step 4

Assignment 20

Hopper

This exercise involves creating a hopper:

(a) as a 3D wire-frame model
(b) as a 3D faced-surface model.

1. Set a two viewport configuration with the viewpoints:
   (a) from above, e.g. VPOINT-ROTATE with 300 and 30
   (b) from below, e.g. VPOINT-ROTATE with 300 and –30.
2. Draw the hopper as a wire-frame model using the sizes given.
3. Add 3D faces to each of the 16 surfaces and colour these surfaces:
   (a) top vertical square: red
   (b) slopes: blue
   (c) small square: yellow
   (d) larger square: green.
4. Hide and shade the model.

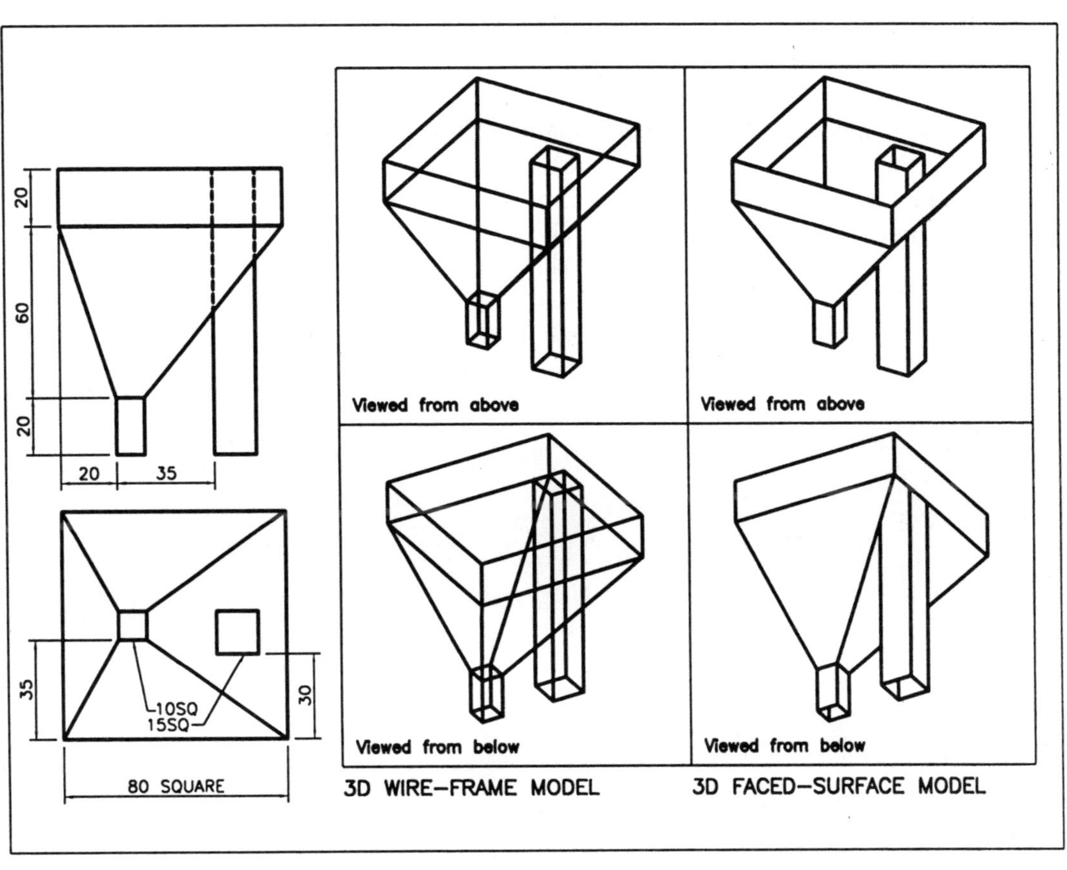
20
60
20
20
35
35
10SQ
15SQ
30
80 SQUARE
Viewed from above
Viewed from above
Viewed from below
Viewed from below
3D WIRE-FRAME MODEL
3D FACED-SURFACE MODEL

Assignment 21

Template drawing

The component has to be drawn and fully dimensioned.

The drawing requires some thought to complete, and adding the dimensions will really test your ability.

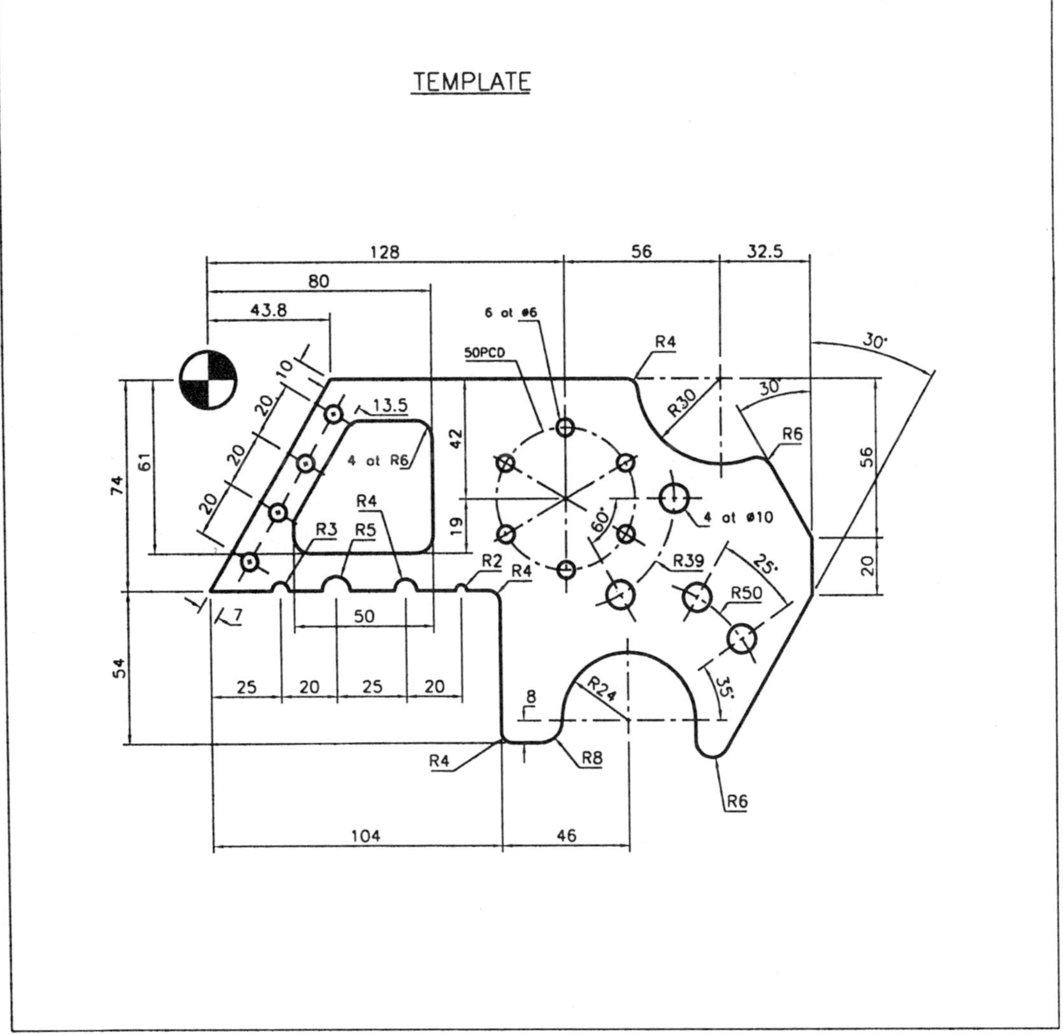
TEMPLATE
128
56
32.5
80
43.8
6 at ø6
50PCD
R4
30°
30°
10
20
20
20
13.5
4 at R6
42
R30
R6
56
74
61
R4
19
60°
4 at ø10
R3
R5
R39
25°
20
R2
R4
R50
7
50
54
25
20
25
20
8
R24
35°
R4
R8
R6
104
46

Assignment 22

Machine guard

Component to be drawn in third angle projection. All hatching, text and dimensions have to be added on the correct layer.

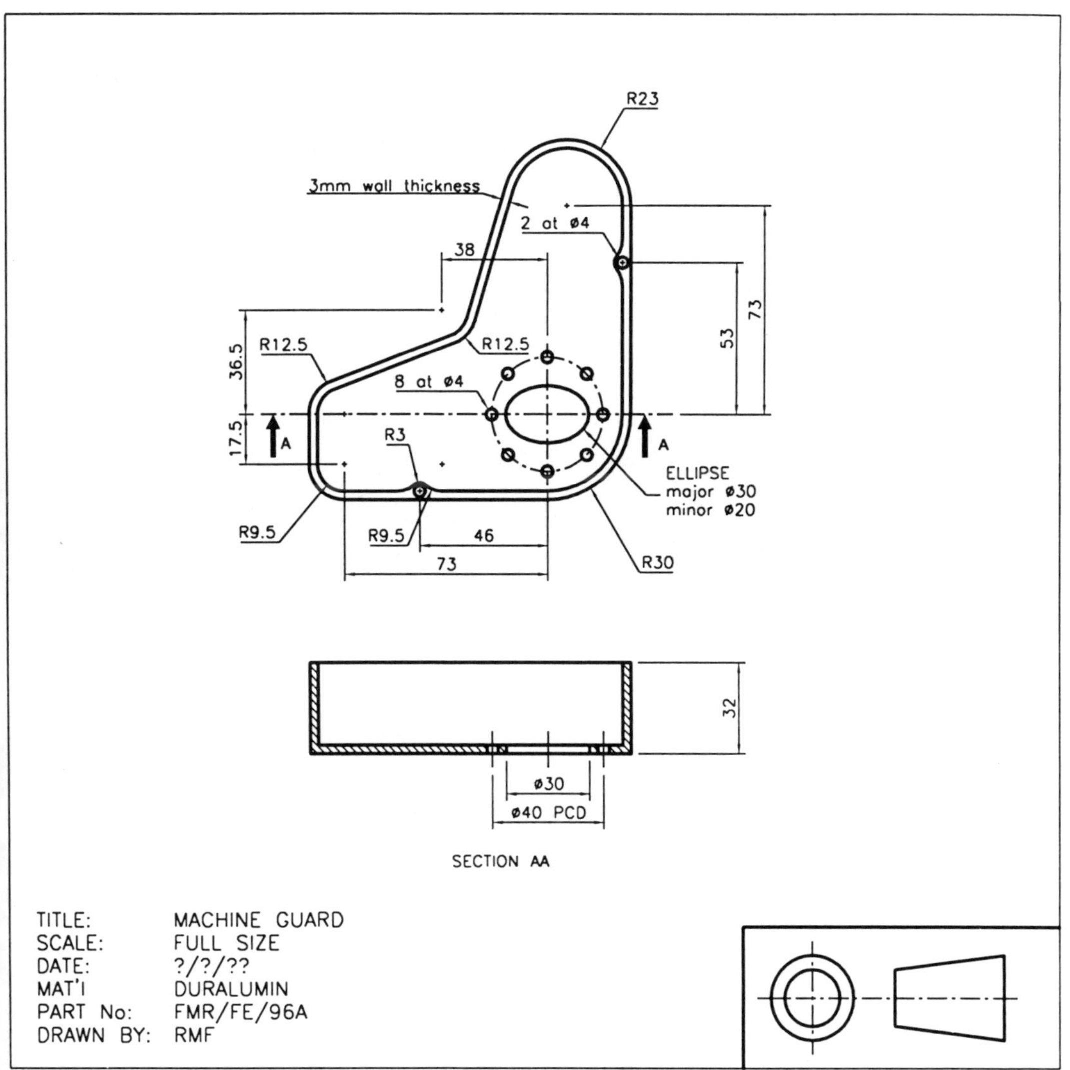
R23
3mm wall thickness
2 at ø4
38
73
53
36.5
R12.5
R12.5
8 at ø4
17.5
A
A
R3
ELLIPSE
major ø30
minor ø20
R9.5
R9.5
46
73
R30
32
ø30
ø40 PCD
SECTION AA
TITLE: MACHINE GUARD
SCALE: FULL SIZE
DATE: ?/?/??
MAT'l DURALUMIN
PART No: FMR/FE/96A
DRAWN BY: RMF

Assignment 23

Support bracket

The component has to:

(a) be drawn as sections on XX and YY as shown.
(b) have all text and dimensions added.

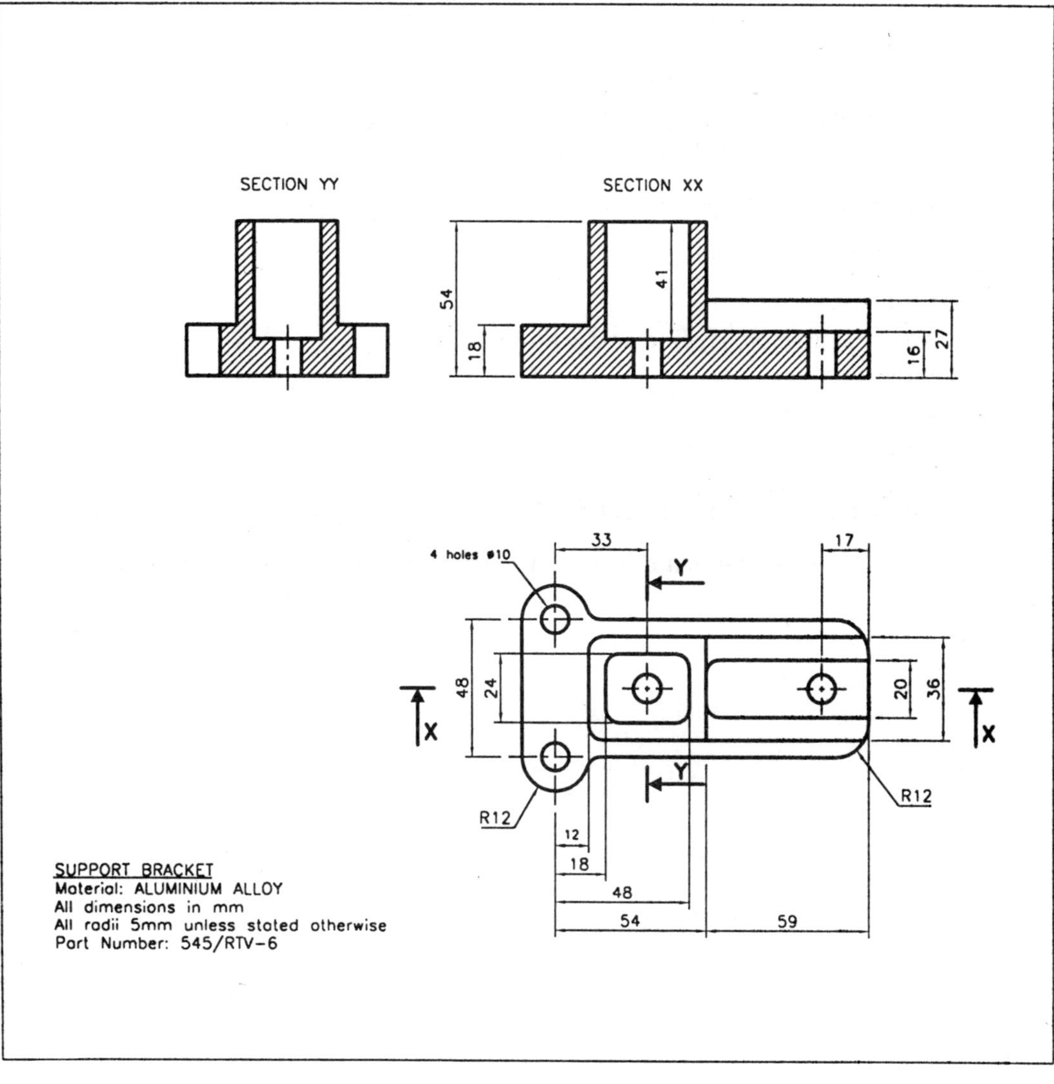
SECTION YY
SECTION XX
54
18
41
16
27
4 holes ø10
33
17
Y
Y
X
X
48
24
20
36
R12
R12
12
18
48
54
59
SUPPORT BRACKET
Material: ALUMINIUM ALLOY
All dimensions in mm
All radii 5mm unless stated otherwise
Part Number: 545/RTV-6

Assignment 24

Leaf

The regular and offset patterns have to be created from the basic leaf shape, using the grid as a reference.

The grid and snap settings are both 10.

The commands used are:

LINE
ARC: Centre, Start, End and 3 Point
MIRROR
SCALE: 0.25
TRIM
SOLID
ARRAY or MULTIPLE COPY

If the ARRAY command is used, the row and column distances are ... ?

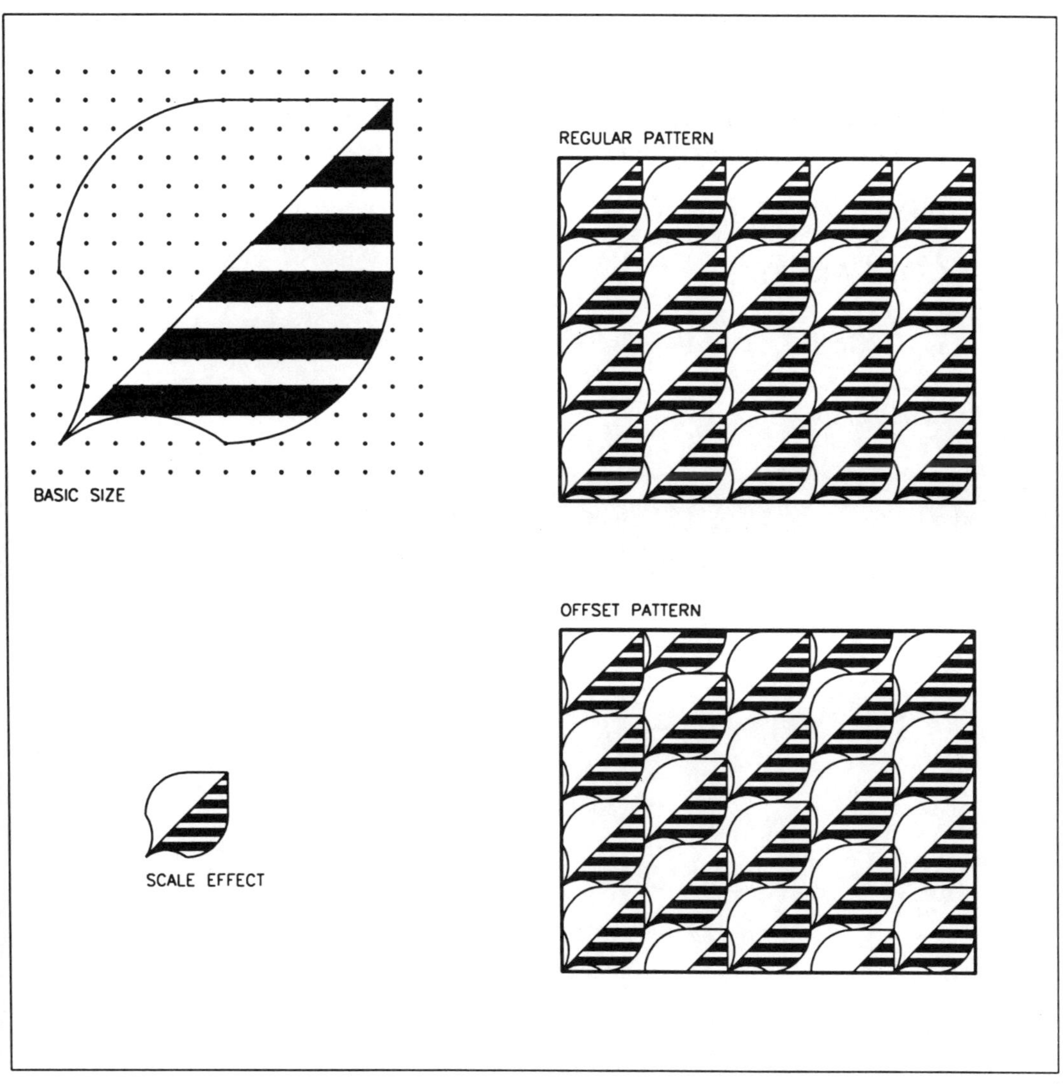
REGULAR PATTERN
BASIC SIZE
OFFSET PATTERN
SCALE EFFECT

Assignment 25

Aztec

With the grid and snap set to 5, create the full size and half size Aztec patterns. The commands are:

LINE
MIRROR
COPY/ARRAY

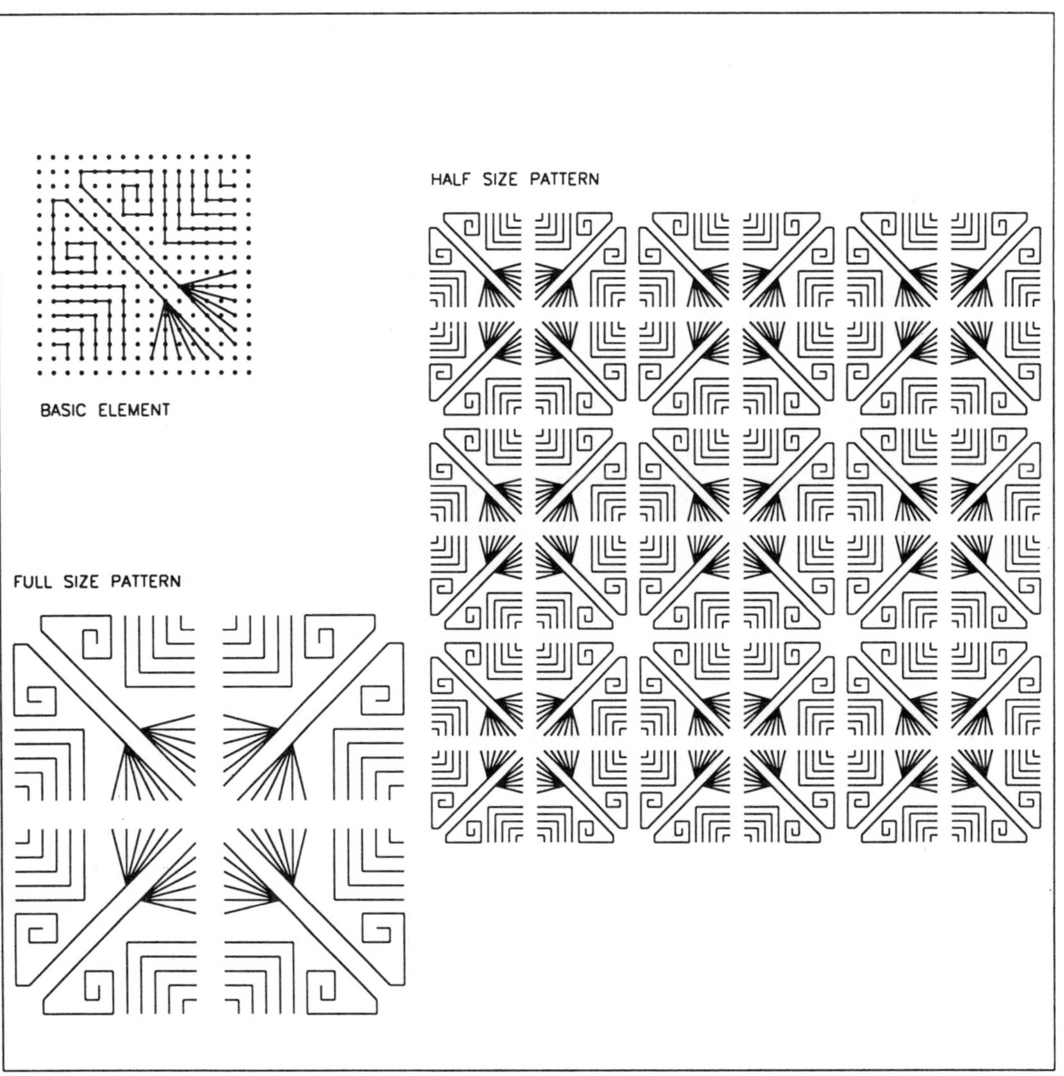

HALF SIZE PATTERN
BASIC ELEMENT
FULL SIZE PATTERN

Assignment 26

Map

Set the grid and snap to 10 and draw the outline map of mainland Britain. Save this drawing as MAP, as it will be used in a later assignment.

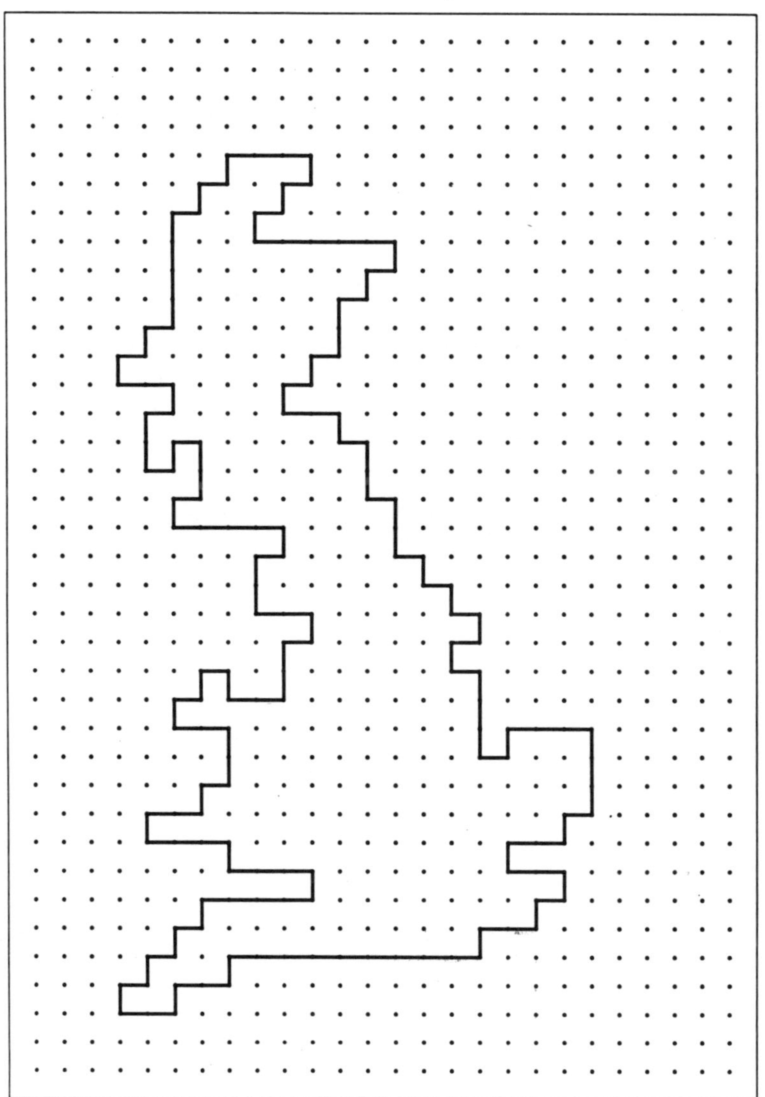

Assignment 27

Nozzle

Sectional view of a component which has to be drawn with text and dimensions added.

The component can be created by different methods – OFFSET/TRIM, MIRROR.

The hatching is ANSI33, but the scale factor value is ... ?

The dimensions take longer than expected.

Part name: NOZZLE
Part number: FG1/56A–C
Material: Mild Steel
Scale: Full size

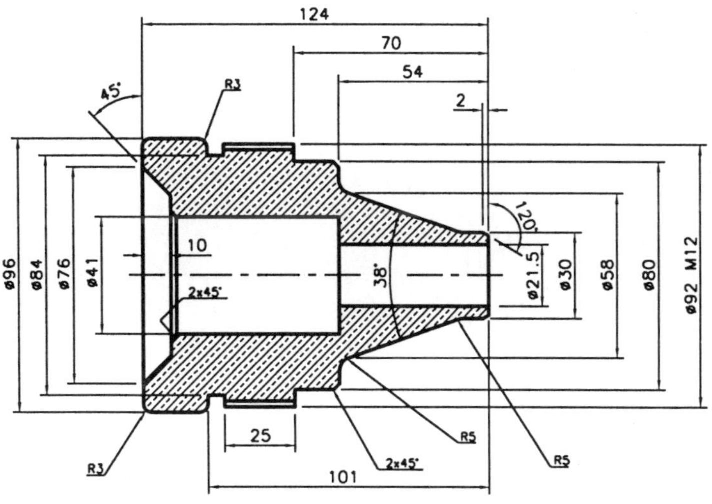

NB: Hatch pattern: ANSI33
Scale: ??

Assignment 28

Swiss mechanism drive

A typical engineering drawing which is easier to complete than you would expect. Polar array is obviously used.

The dimensions should give no problems.

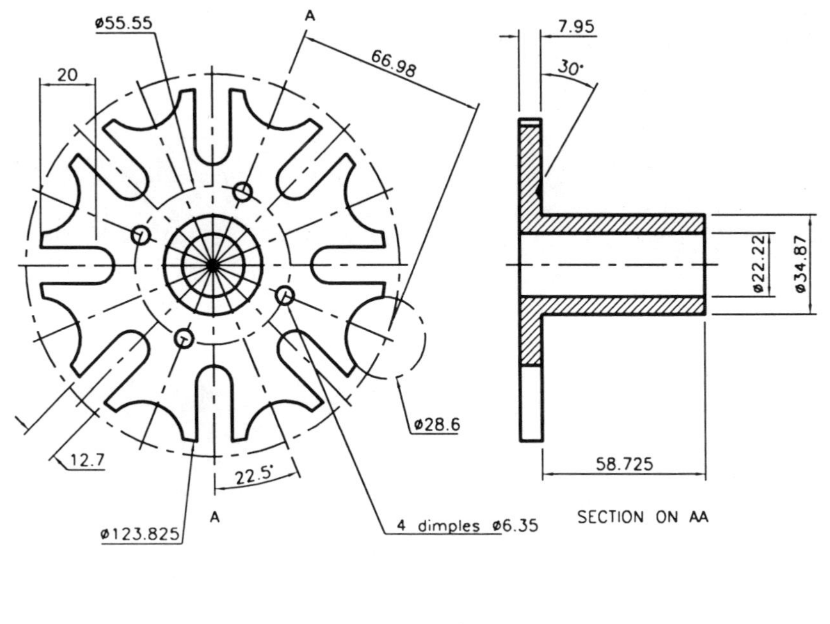
SWISS MECHANISM DRIVE
ø55.55
A
66.98
20
7.95
30°
ø22.22
ø34.87
ø28.6
12.7
22.5°
58.725
A
ø123.825
4 dimples ø6.35
SECTION ON AA

Assignment 29

Rivets

In this exercise the rivets have to be drawn accurately using the data given for each type.

I set the value of L to 110 and D to 20.

The dimensions have to be added to all rivets with a text style of ROMANT at a height of 3.

The text is:

(a) Rivet name: ITALICT at height 5
(b) Data: SCRIPTC at height 4.

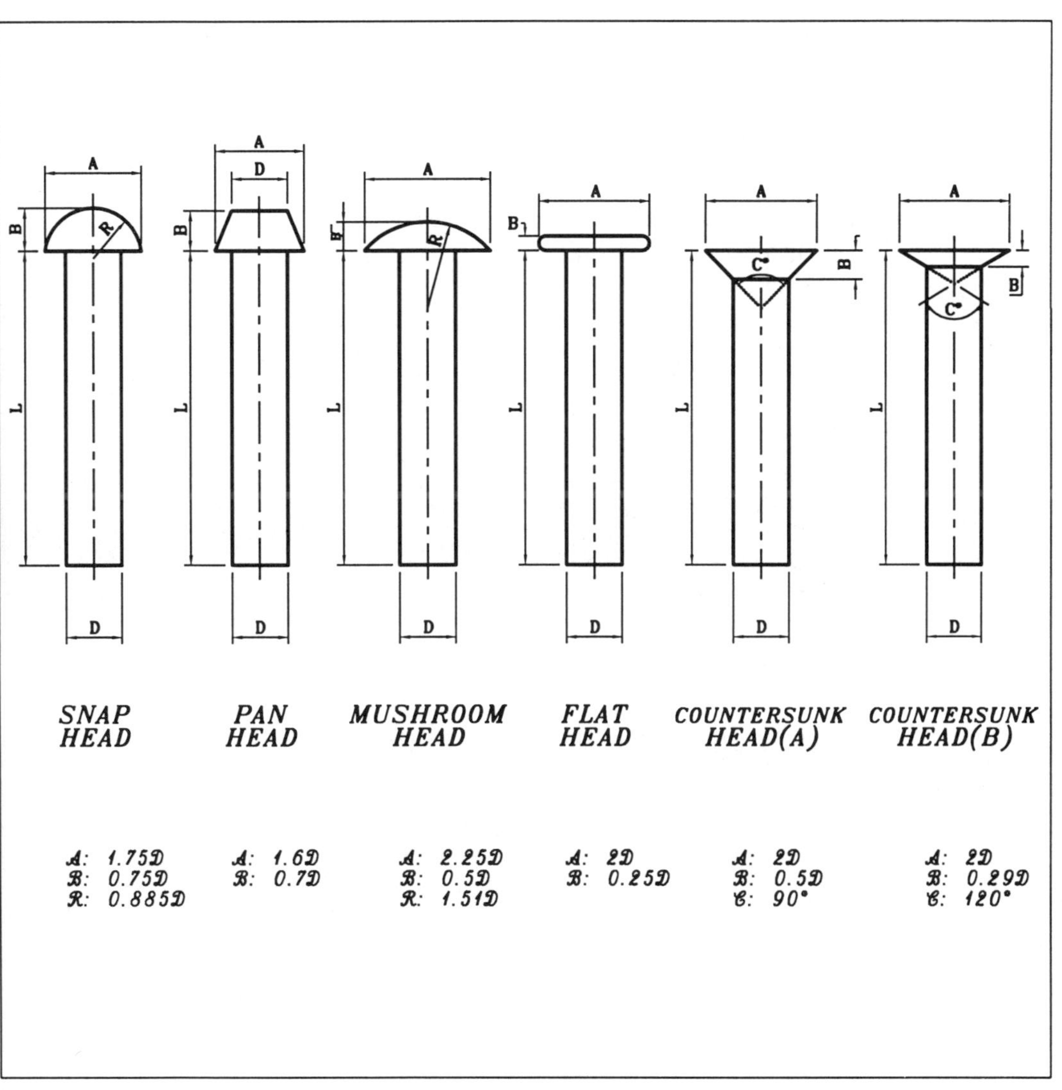
A
D
B
L
R
C°
SNAP HEAD
PAN HEAD
MUSHROOM HEAD
FLAT HEAD
COUNTERSUNK HEAD(A)
COUNTERSUNK HEAD(B)
A: 1.75D
B: 0.75D
R: 0.885D
A: 1.6D
B: 0.7D
A: 2.25D
B: 0.5D
R: 1.51D
A: 2D
B: 0.25D
A: 2D
B: 0.5D
C: 90°
A: 2D
B: 0.29D
C: 120°

Assignment 30

Can you tolerate it?

Two components to be drawn and dimensioned.

You can:

(a) alter the various dimension variables
(b) set different dimension styles.

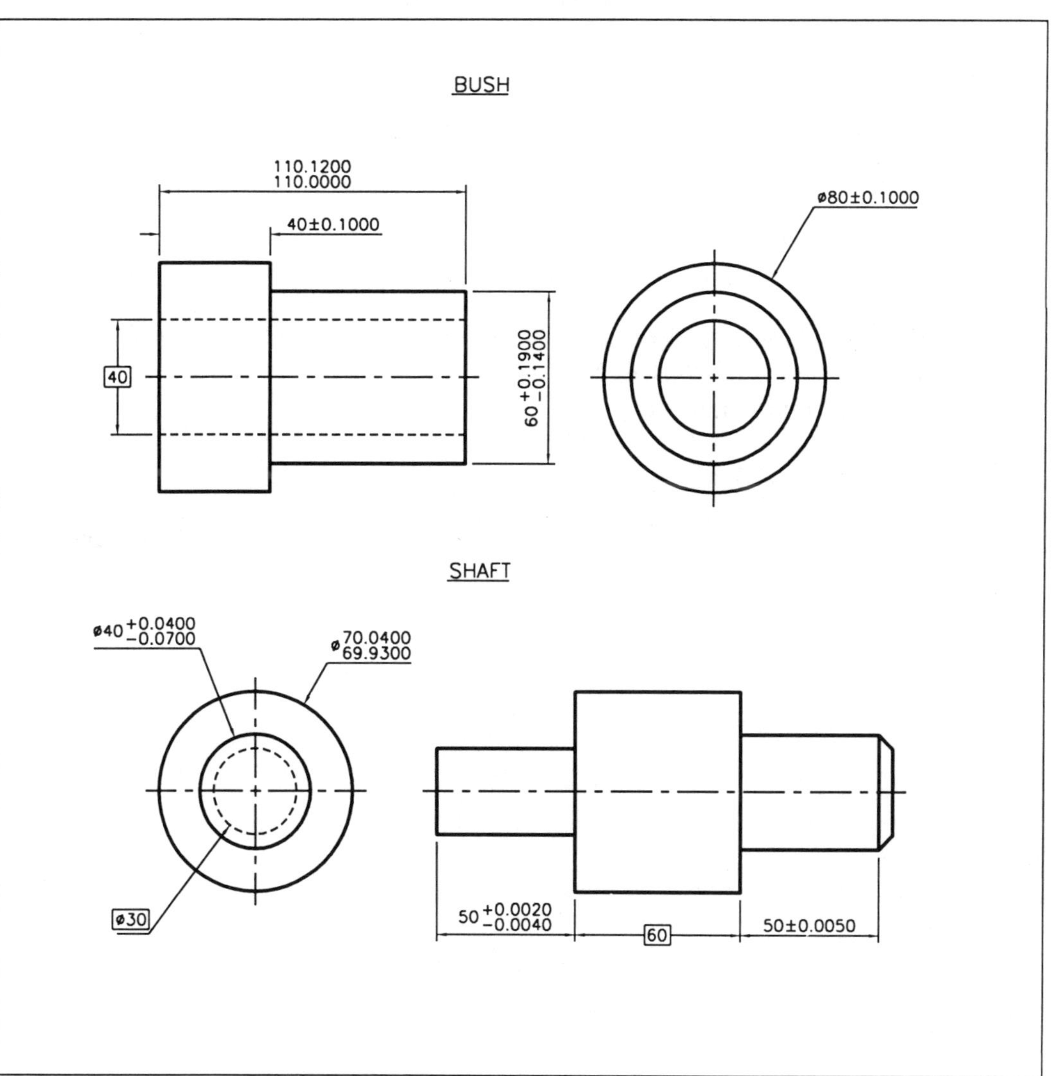
BUSH
110.1200
110.0000
40±0.1000
ø80±0.1000
40
60 +0.1900 −0.1400
SHAFT
ø40 +0.0400 −0.0700
ø 70.0400 69.9300
ø30
50 +0.0020 −0.0040
60
50±0.0050

Assignment 31

Boss pipe

This assignment requires the MVSETUP command to be used with:

(a) units: decimal
(b) scale: 2
(c) paper width: 600
(d) paper height: 424.

All dimensions and text have to be added.
Note: (1) value of dimscale?
(2) text height values?

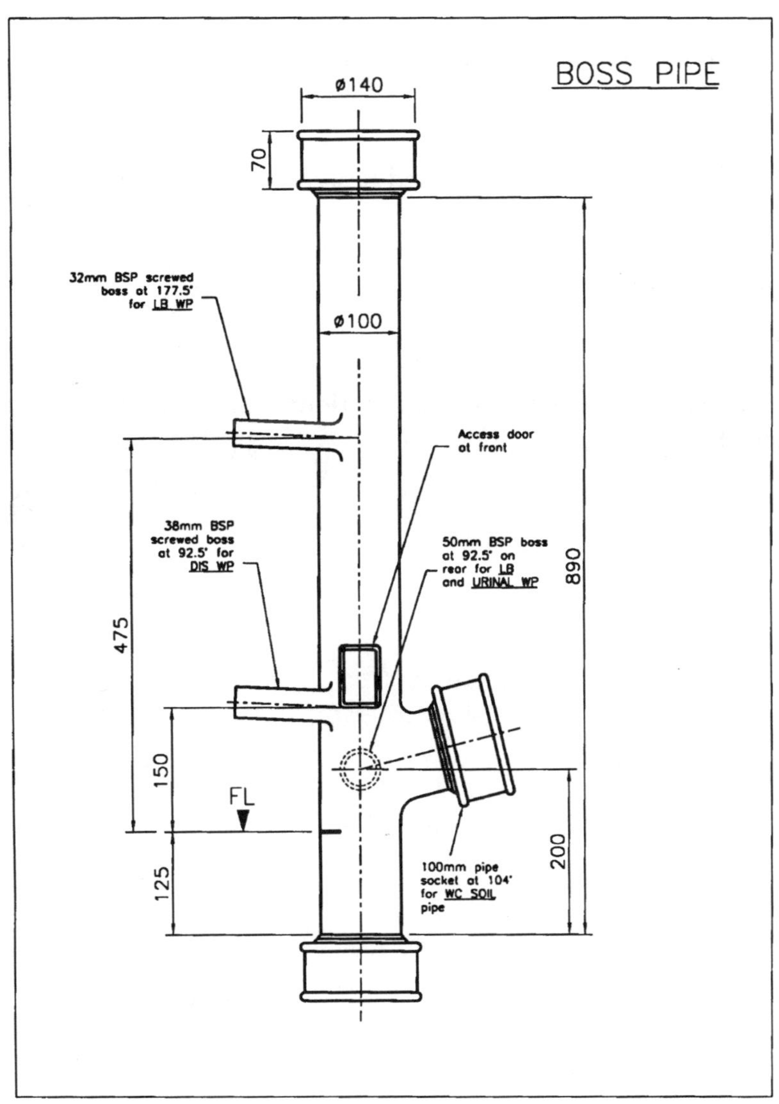
BOSS PIPE
ø140
70
32mm BSP screwed
boss at 177.5°
for LB WP
ø100
Access door
at front
38mm BSP
screwed boss
at 92.5° for
DIS WP
50mm BSP boss
at 92.5° on
rear for LB
and URINAL WP
890
475
150
FL
125
200
100mm pipe
socket at 104°
for WC SOIL
pipe

Assignment 32

Isometric bush

1. This component has been drawn with the LIMITS set:
   (a) from 0, 0
   (b) to 11, 9.
2. The dimensions have to be added as shown, and I altered the following dimension variables:
   dimtad: 0, i.e. OFF
   dimtvp: 0
   dimtih: 1, i.e. ON
   dimscale: 0.035
3. A complete isometric view and a sectional isometric view have to be added.

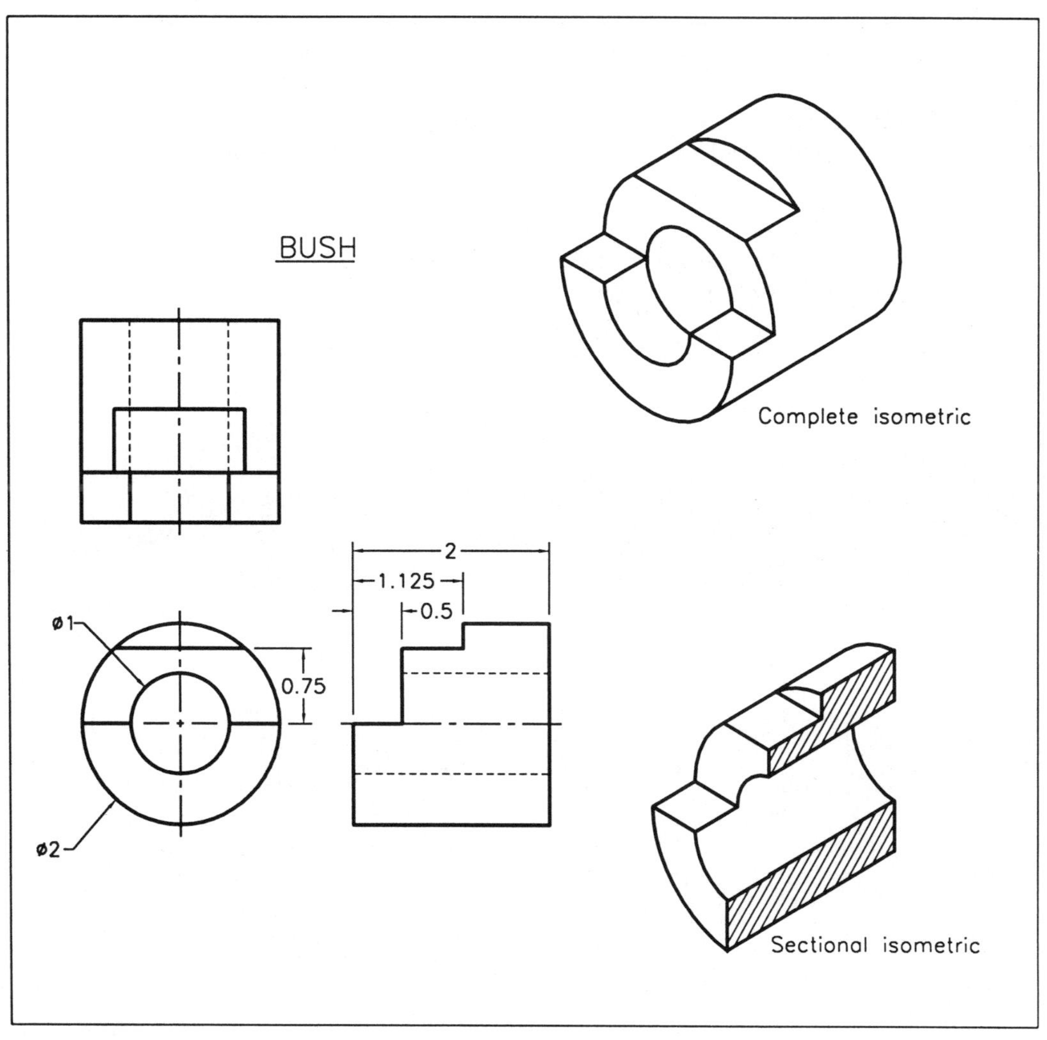
BUSH
Complete isometric
2
1.125
0.5
Ø1
0.75
Ø2
Sectional isometric

Assignment 33

Just a brick in the wall

Create the garden wall from the following:

(a) set the grid and snap to 5, and draw the basic shape
(b) mirror the basic shape
(c) scale by 0.2
(d) array or multiple copy to complete the wall
(e) add any 'refinements'.

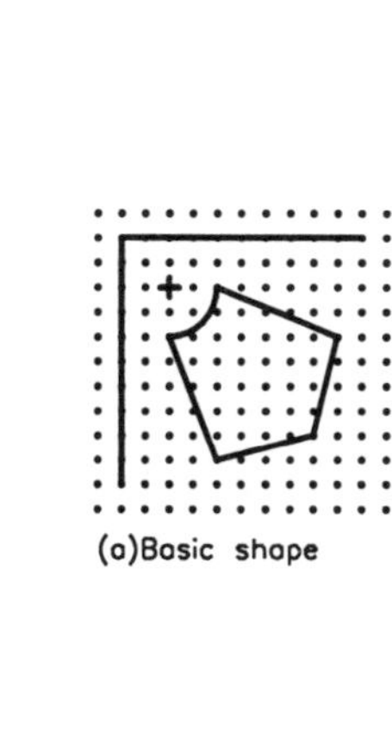
(a)Basic shape

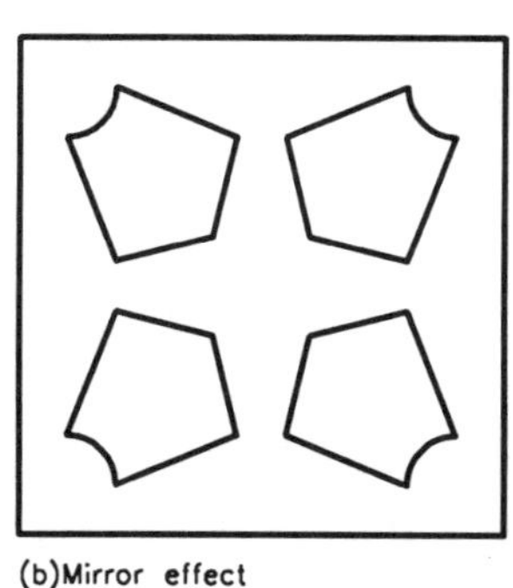
(b)Mirror effect

(c)Scale factor 0.2

COMPLETED WALL

Assignment 34

Another brick in the wall

Create an isometric ornamental wall effect by:

(a) grid and snap set to 10
(b) draw the basic shape
(c) scale effect of 0.25
(d) complete the wall – array or multiple copy?

Note: there is a 'double' isometric effect.

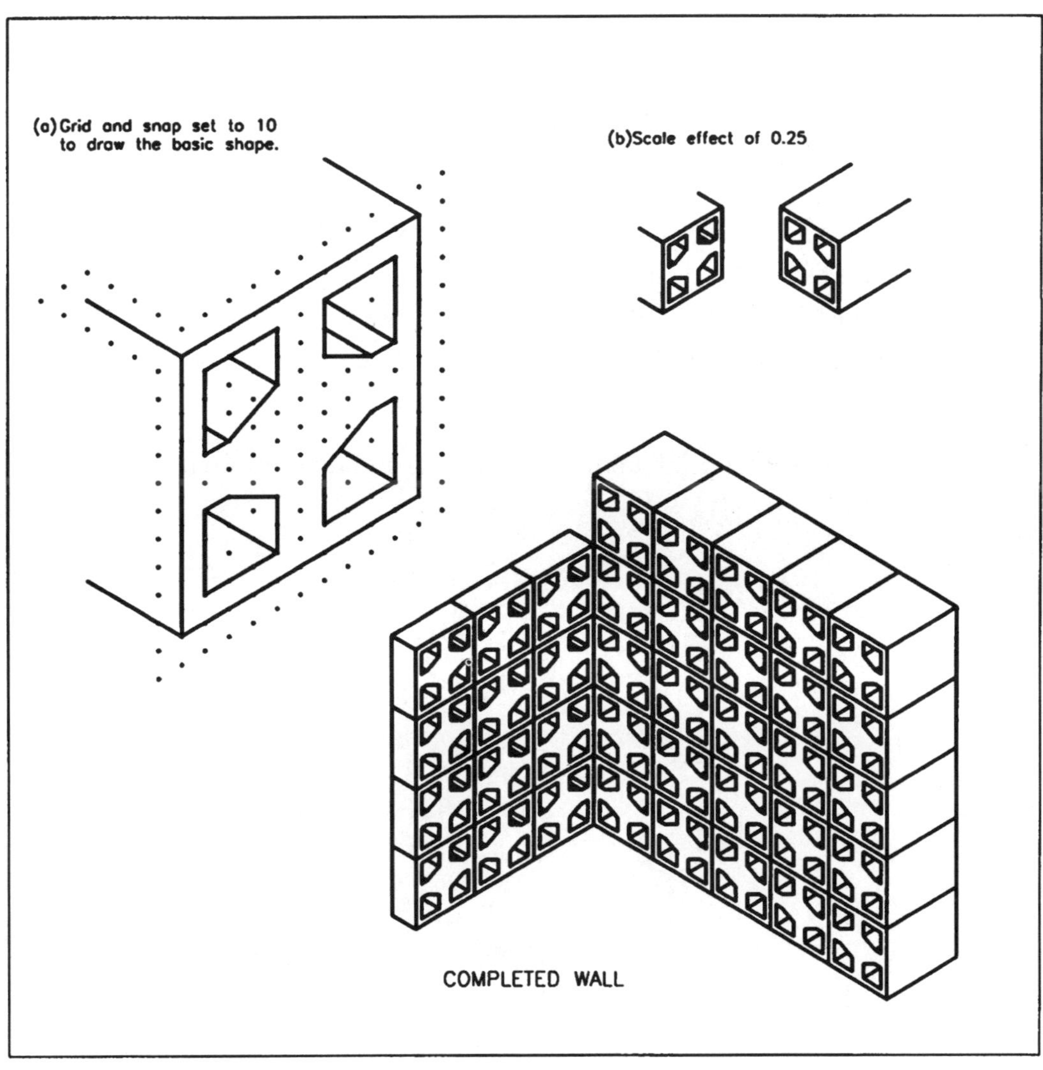
(a) Grid and snap set to 10
to draw the basic shape.
(b)Scale effect of 0.25
COMPLETED WALL

Assignment 35

Weather map

1. Open your MAP drawing from Assignment 26.
2. Zoom in on a blank area of the screen.
3. Draw the seven weather symbols using a grid/snap of 5.
4. Make a block of each symbol, using the name given. The block insertion point is at your discretion.
5. Insert the blocks to produce a weather map, adding any modifications of your choice.

Note: the block insertion points, scale factors and rotation are for you to decide.

54
35
19
24
25
33
27
29
15
28
32
5

Assignment 36

Positioning block 1

Using the sizes given, draw:

(a) the three orthographic views
(b) an isometric as shown.

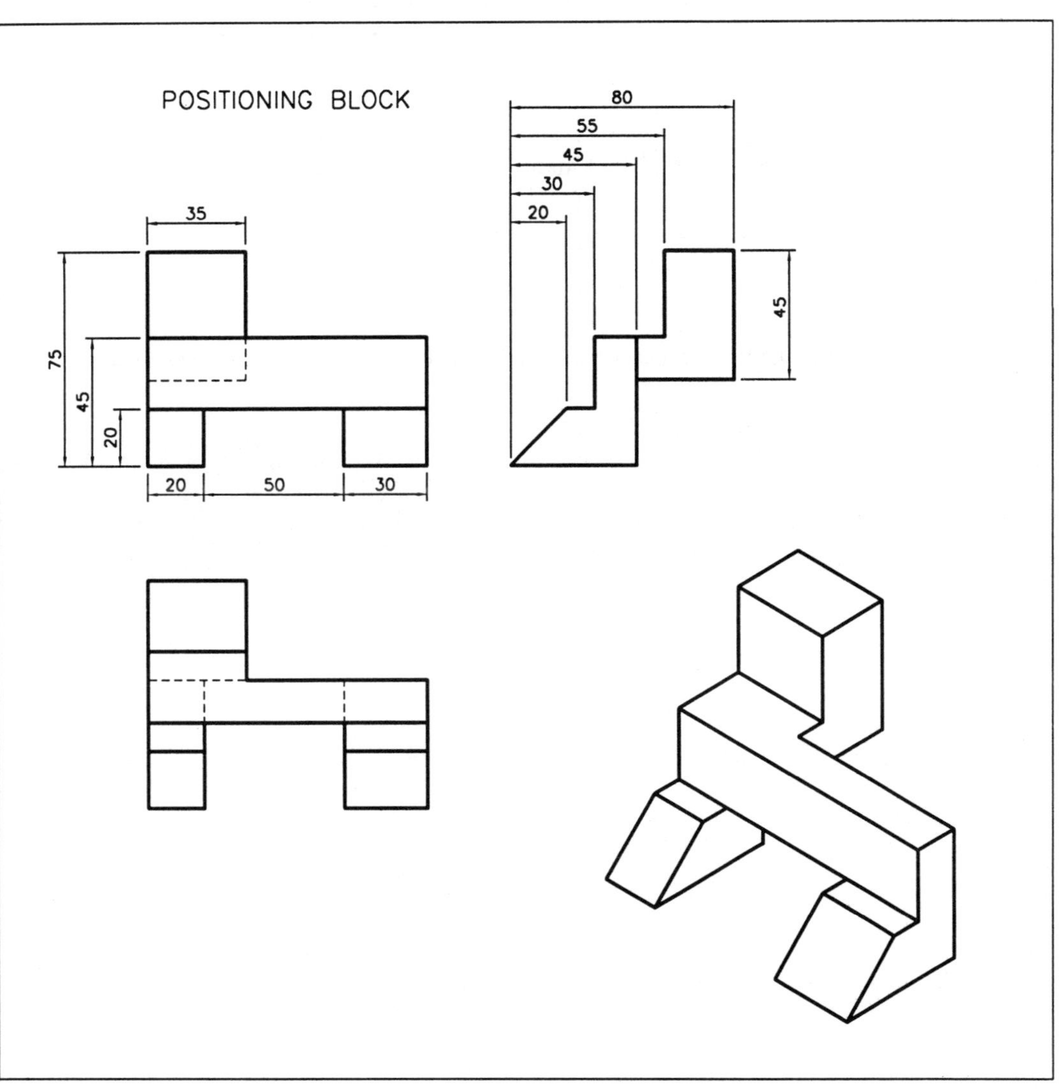
POSITIONING BLOCK
35
75
45
20
20
50
30
80
55
45
30
20
45

Assignment 37

Positioning block 2

Create a paper-space two viewport configuration and draw a wire-frame model of the positioning block using the sizes from assignment 36, then:

(a) add the dimensions to the left viewport
(b) hatch the surface in the right viewport as given.

Notes

1. UCS positions need to be set and saved for both the dimensions and the hatching.
2. **Take great care with the hatch scale.**

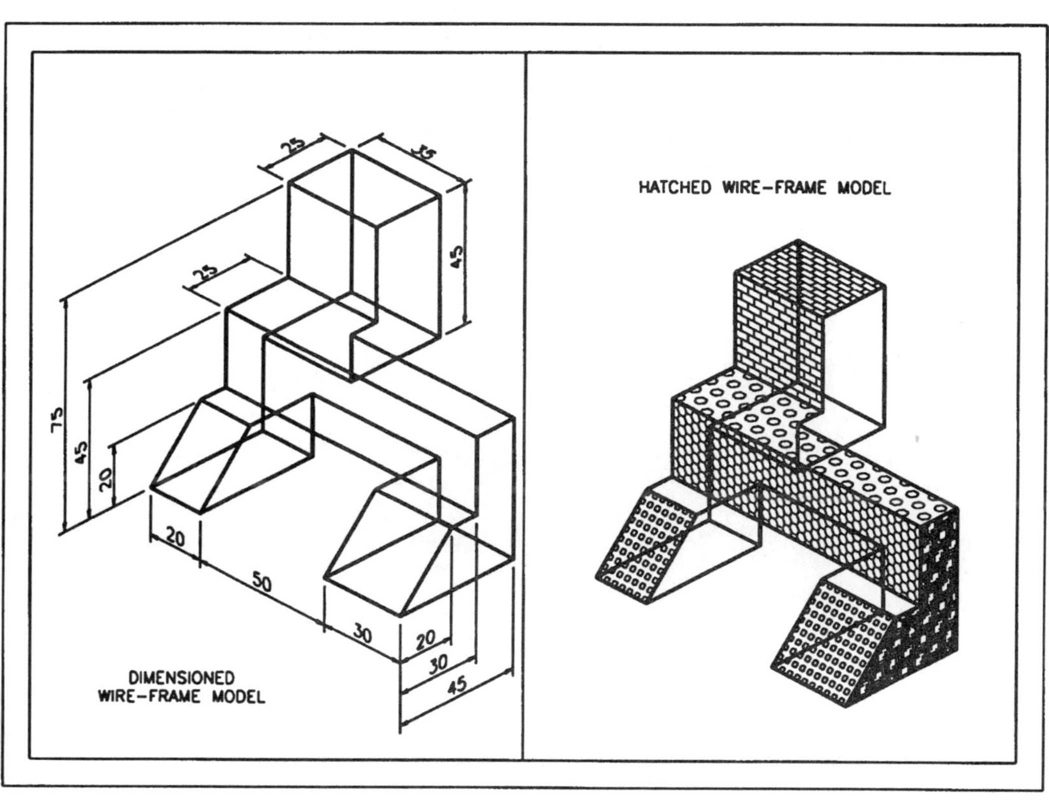
25
35
45
25
75
45
20
20
50
30
20
30
45
DIMENSIONED
WIRE-FRAME MODEL
HATCHED WIRE-FRAME MODEL

Assignment 38

Two components

The two components have to be drawn and fully dimensioned.

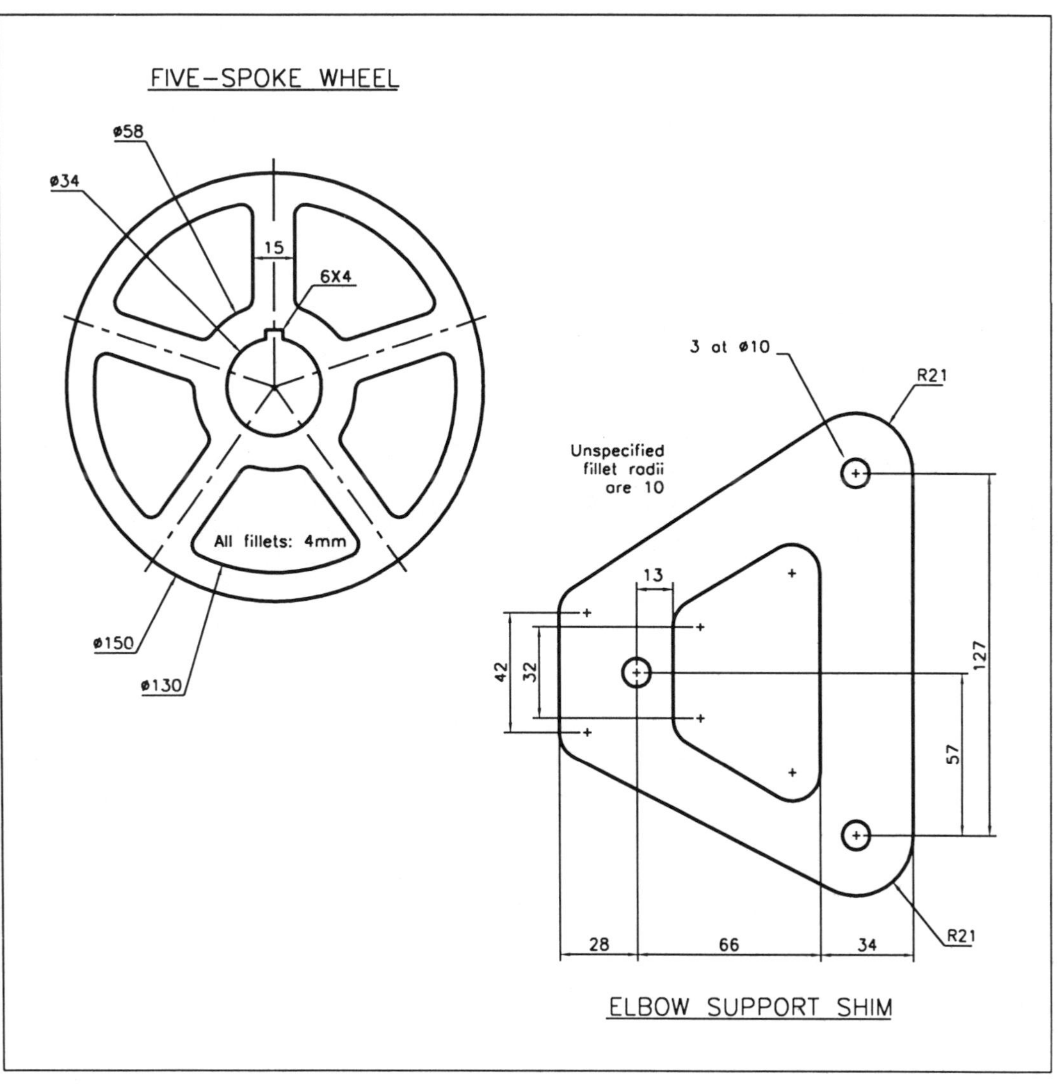
FIVE-SPOKE WHEEL
ø58
ø34
15
6X4
All fillets: 4mm
ø150
ø130
3 at ø10
R21
Unspecified
fillet radii
are 10
13
42
32
127
57
R21
28
66
34
ELBOW SUPPORT SHIM

Assignment 39

Serial interface

Draw the circuit as shown.

No sizes are given, so you will need to use your skill with the layout.

I used middle text for the numbers in the 'boxes' and set the grid to 10 and the snap to 5.

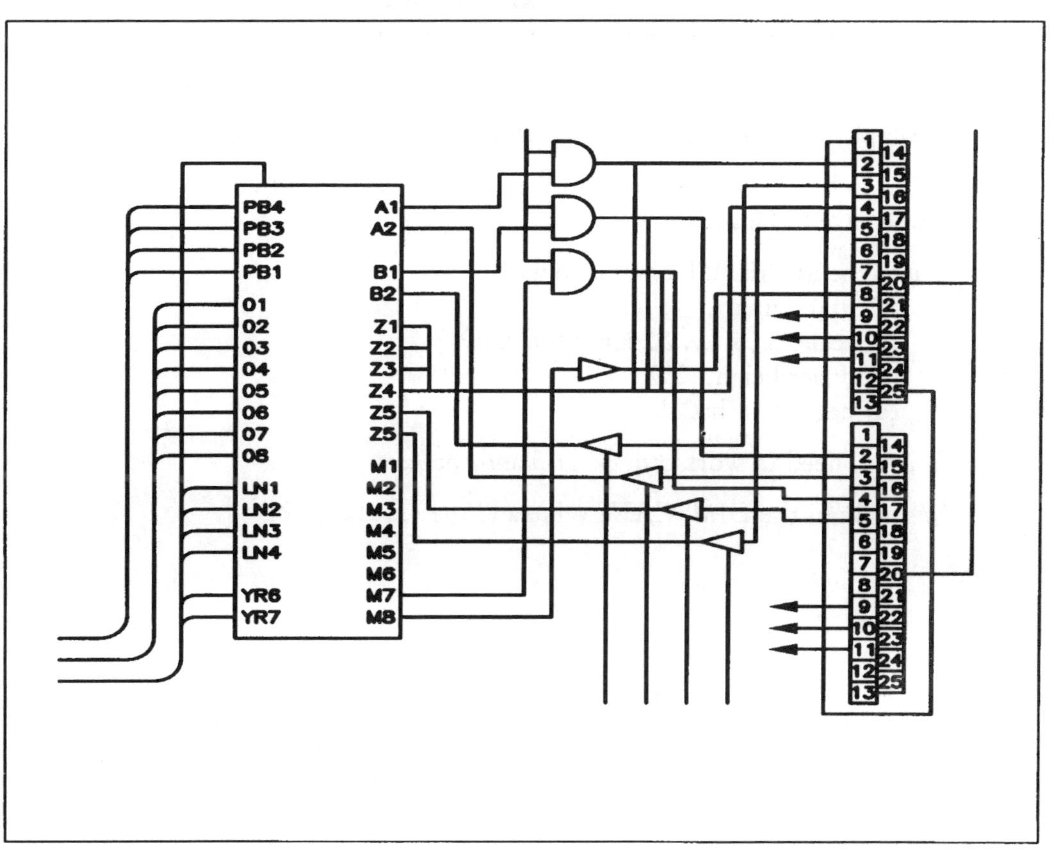
PB4
PB3
PB2
PB1
01
02
03
04
05
06
07
08
LN1
LN2
LN3
LN4
YR6
YR7
A1
A2
B1
B2
Z1
Z2
Z3
Z4
Z5
Z5
M1
M2
M3
M4
M5
M6
M7
M8

Assignment 40

Brake shoe

A simple drawing which is more complex than it would appear.

It has to be drawn at 20 times full-size on A4 paper. All dimensions and a title have to be added.

I used the MVSETUP command with:

(a) units: metric
(b) scale: 0.05, i.e. 20 times full size?
(c) paper height: 297
(d) paper width: 210

You will need to work out the grid and snap settings.

What about the DIMSCALE value and the text height?

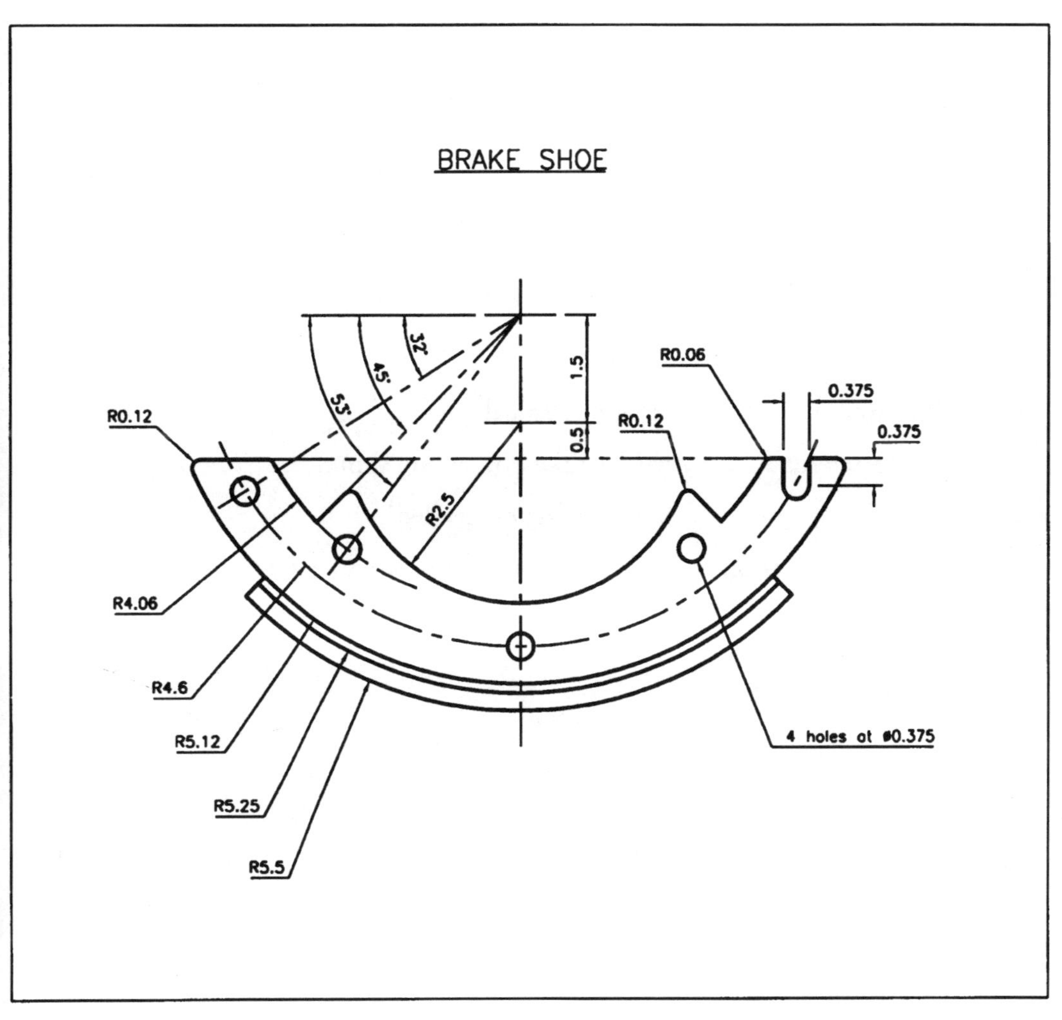
BRAKE SHOE
32°
45°
53°
1.5
0.5
R0.06
0.375
0.375
R0.12
R0.12
R2.5
R4.06
R4.6
R5.12
R5.25
R5.5
4 holes at ø0.375

Assignment 41

Using engineering units

Three components which have to be drawn and dimensioned using Engineering units with:

(a) precision: four places
(b) grid: 0.5, snap 0.25
(c) limits: 0,0 to 23″,15″
(d) text size?
(e) overall dimension scale value? – think small!

The three components are:

shim:	straightforward
heater tube:	harder than you would think.
	Some tangency needed?
adjusting ring:	much easier than you would expect.

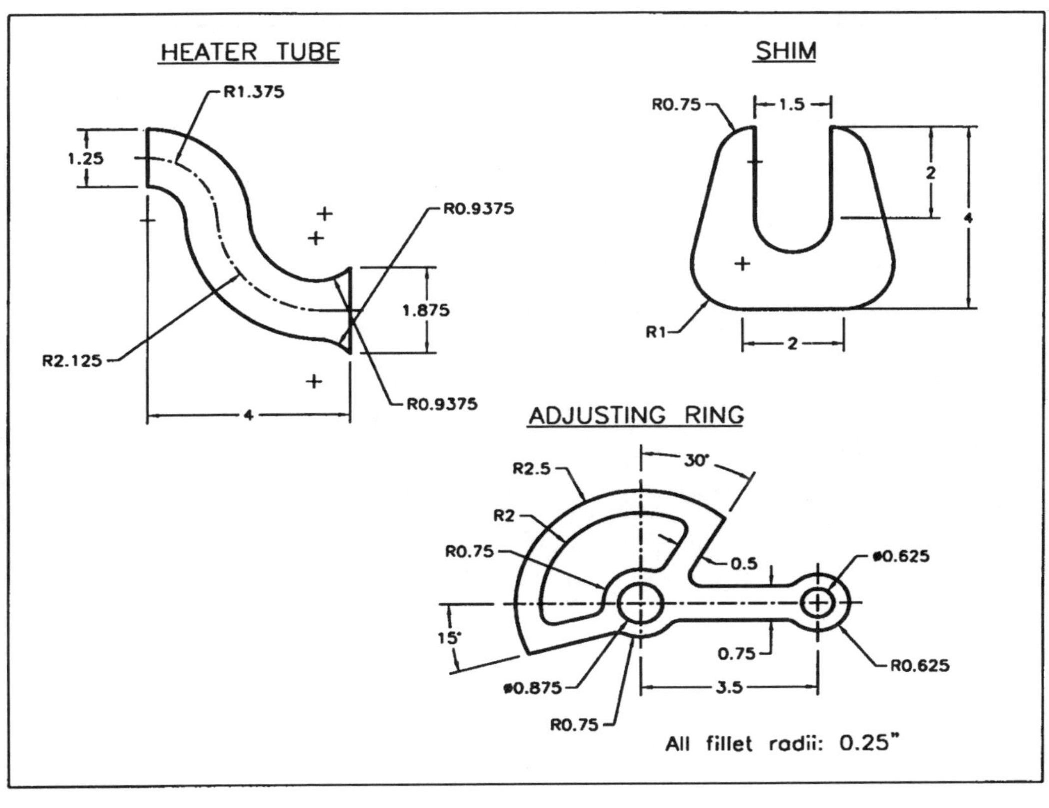
HEATER TUBE
R1.375
1.25
R0.9375
1.875
R2.125
R0.9375
4
SHIM
R0.75
1.5
2
4
R1
2
ADJUSTING RING
R2.5
30°
R2
R0.75
0.5
⌀0.625
15°
0.75
R0.625
⌀0.875
3.5
R0.75
All fillet radii: 0.25"

Assignment 42

3D piping arrangement

A simple drawing to complete – or is it?

You have to draw the 3D piping arrangement as 1-mm wide polylines and polyarcs.

Different UCS positions needed?

The dimensions have to be added as given.

Note
I have shown a three-viewport configuration with a top and front view of the piping set up.

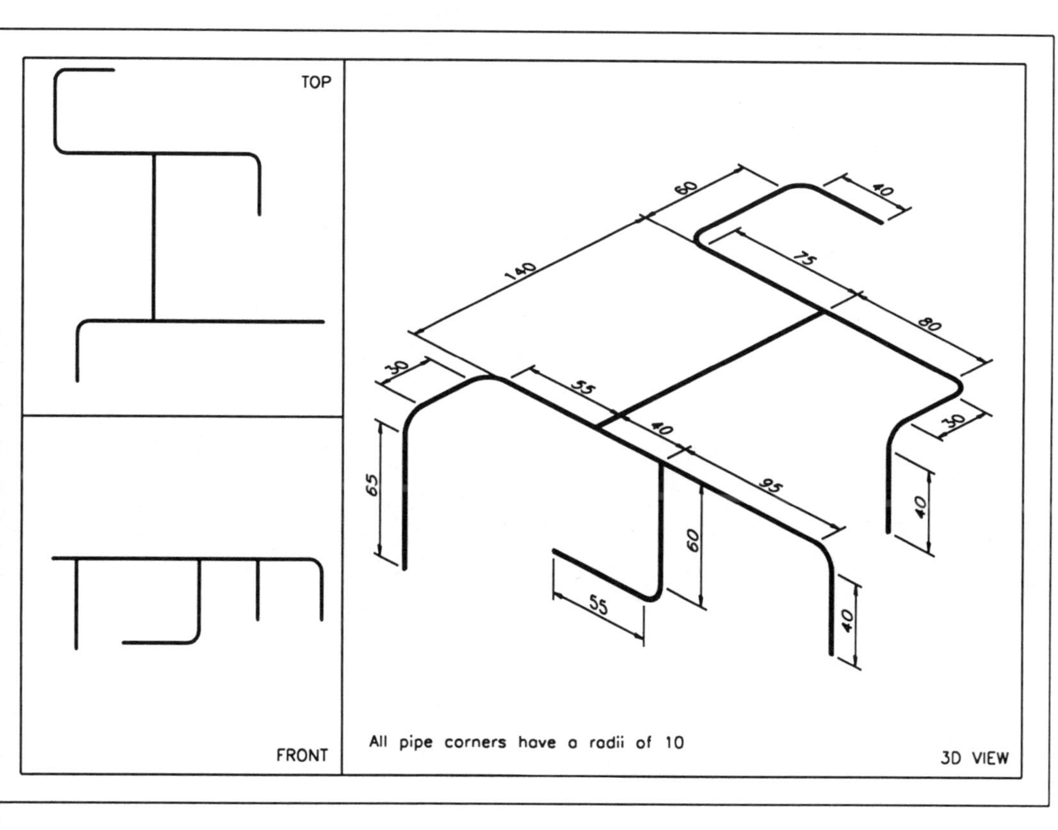
TOP
FRONT
All pipe corners have a radii of 10
3D VIEW
60
40
140
75
80
30
55
30
40
65
95
40
60
55
40

Assignment 43

Isometric 2

Using the information given:

(a) construct the two views
(b) draw the stepped sectional isometric through the given line
(c) add the ORDINATE dimensions.

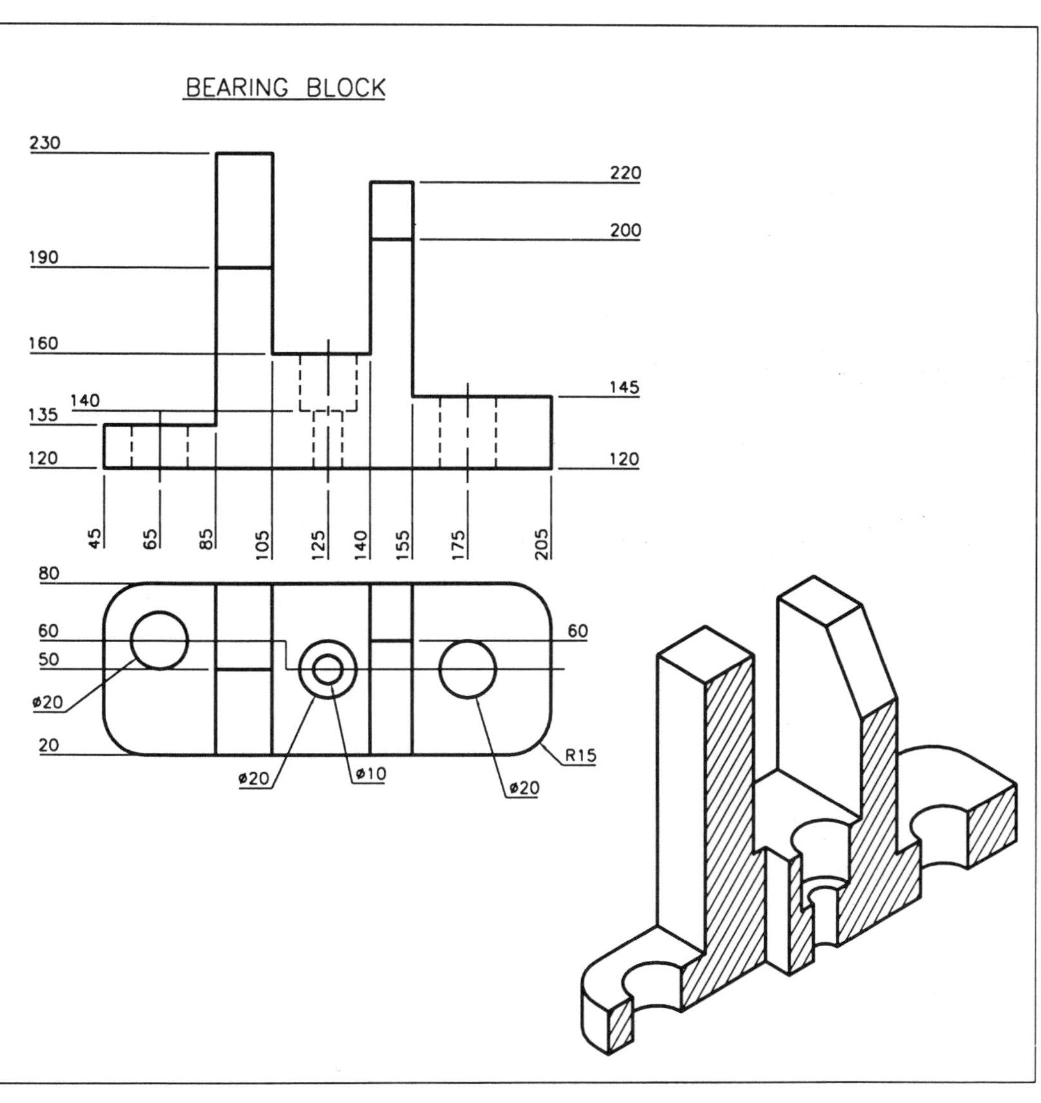
BEARING BLOCK
230
190
160
140
135
120
220
200
145
120
45
65
85
105
125
140
155
175
205
80
60
50
ø20
20
60
R15
ø20
ø10
ø20

Assignment 44

3D wire-frame model

Set a three-viewport configuration, and:

1. draw the three orthographic views of the component
2. create a 3D wire-frame model and display at two different viewports.

Note

(a) current layer frozen required?
(b) rulesurf?

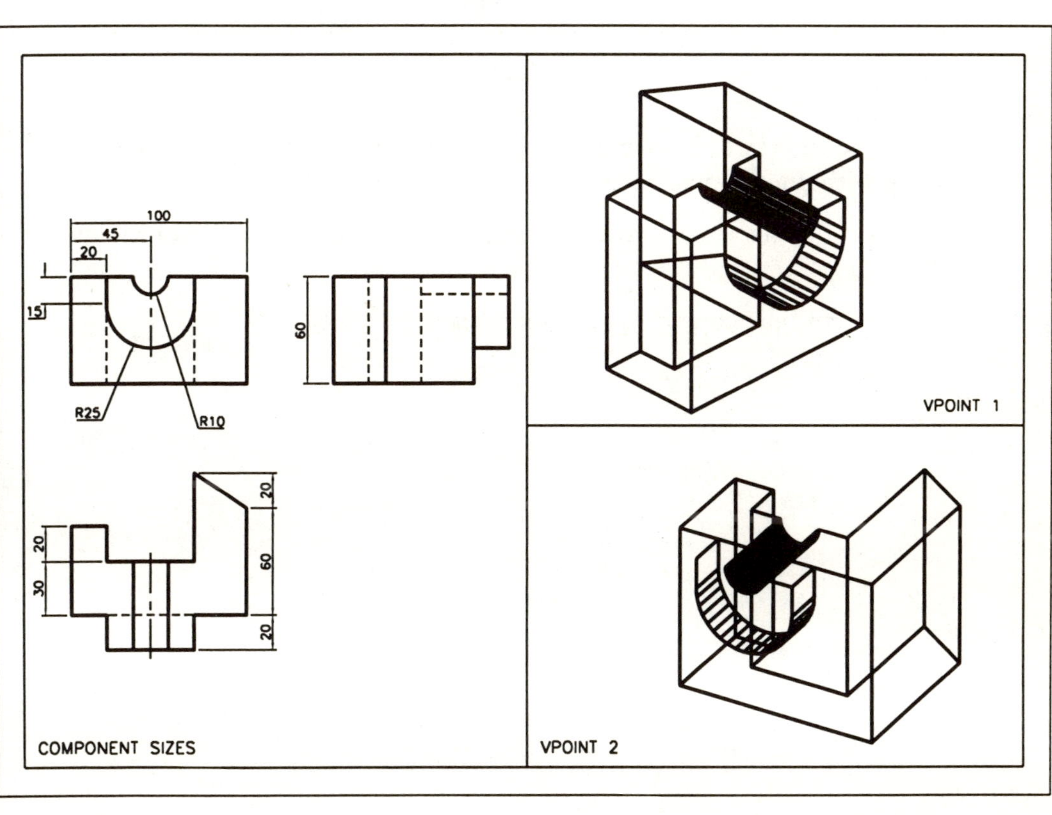
100
45
20
15
60
R25
R10
20
30
20
60
20
COMPONENT SIZES
VPOINT 1
VPOINT 2

Assignment 45

Designs

You have to create the two given designs for the basic shapes which are given with dimensions. Each design is at a scale of 0.5.

The circle radius is 85, and the octagon is inscribed in a circle of radius 85.

Do you multiple copy or rectangular array?

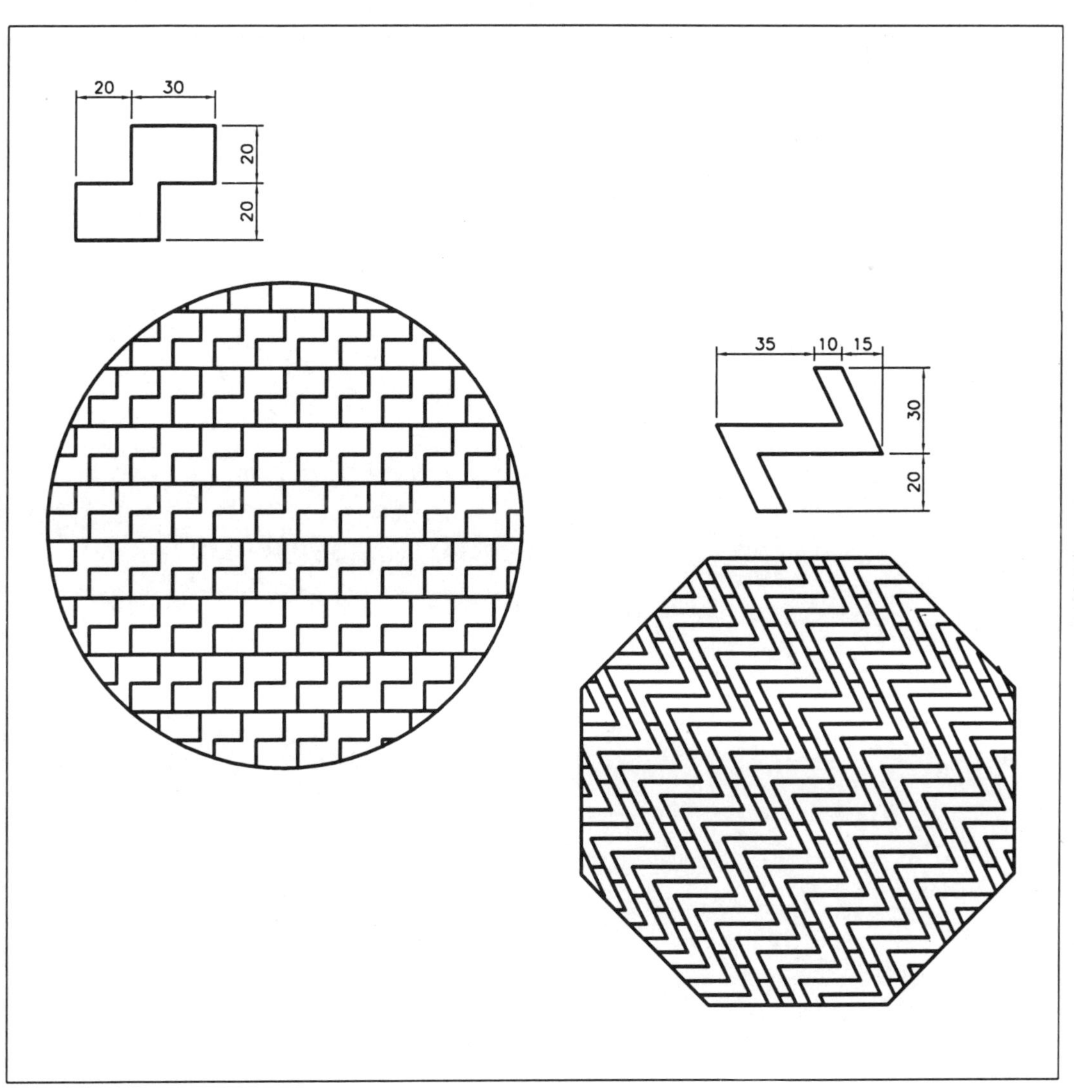

20
30
20
20
35
10
15
30
20

Assignment 46

Two supports

The two supports have to be drawn and fully dimensioned.

No problem, so no help.

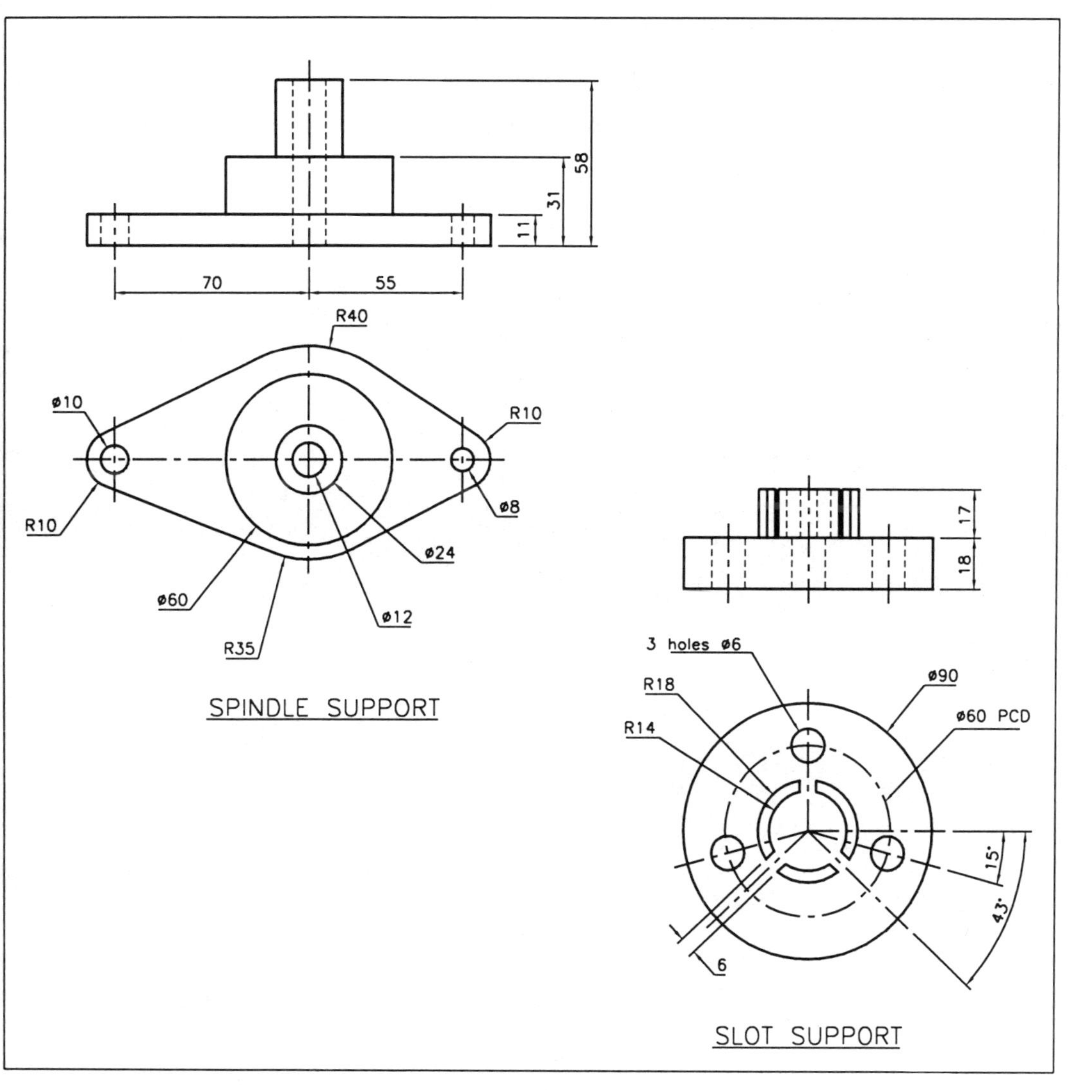
58
31
11
70
55
R40
ø10
R10
R10
ø8
ø24
ø60
ø12
R35
SPINDLE SUPPORT
17
18
3 holes ø6
R18
ø90
R14
ø60 PCD
15°
43°
6
SLOT SUPPORT

Assignment 47

Angle plate

The component has to be drawn full size with **all** dimensions added.

The 'awkward' sizes are deliberate, so no cheating!

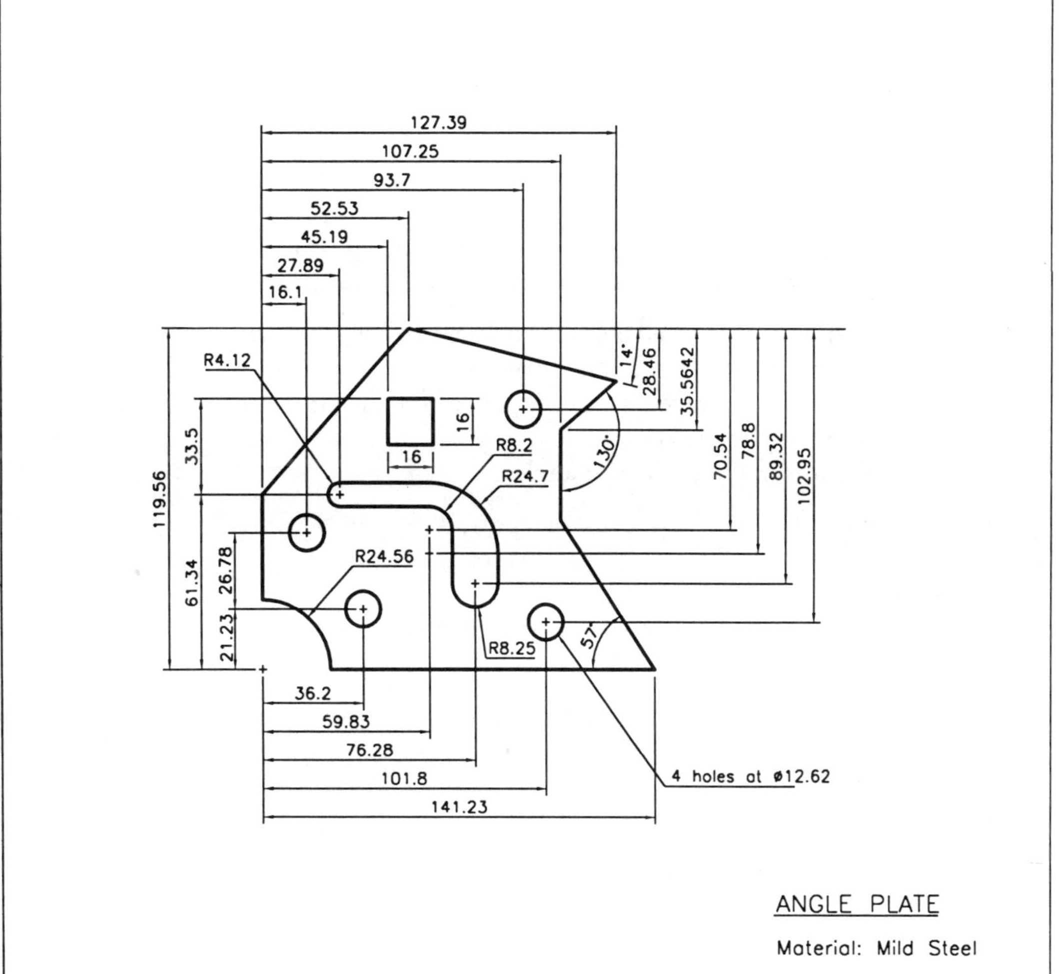
127.39
107.25
93.7
52.53
45.19
27.89
16.1
R4.12
14°
28.46
35.5642
16
16
R8.2
R24.7
130°
70.54
78.8
89.32
102.95
119.56
33.5
61.34
26.78
21.23
R24.56
R8.25
57°
36.2
59.83
76.28
101.8
141.23
4 holes at ø12.62
ANGLE PLATE
Material: Mild Steel

Assignment 48

3D shaft–pulley assembly

For this assignment you have to:

1. set a two-viewport configuration
2. draw a 'centre line'
3. draw the component profile as a continuous polyline, using the given sizes as a reference – you can alter them or use your own design.
4. activate the Revolved Surface command and:
   (a) pick the polyline as the path curve
   (b) pick the 'centre line' as the axis of revolution
   (c) enter 0 as the start angle
   (d) enter ... (?) as the end angle.
5. Remember to HIDE each viewport.

Task
Can you plot the two viewports to give the hide effect?

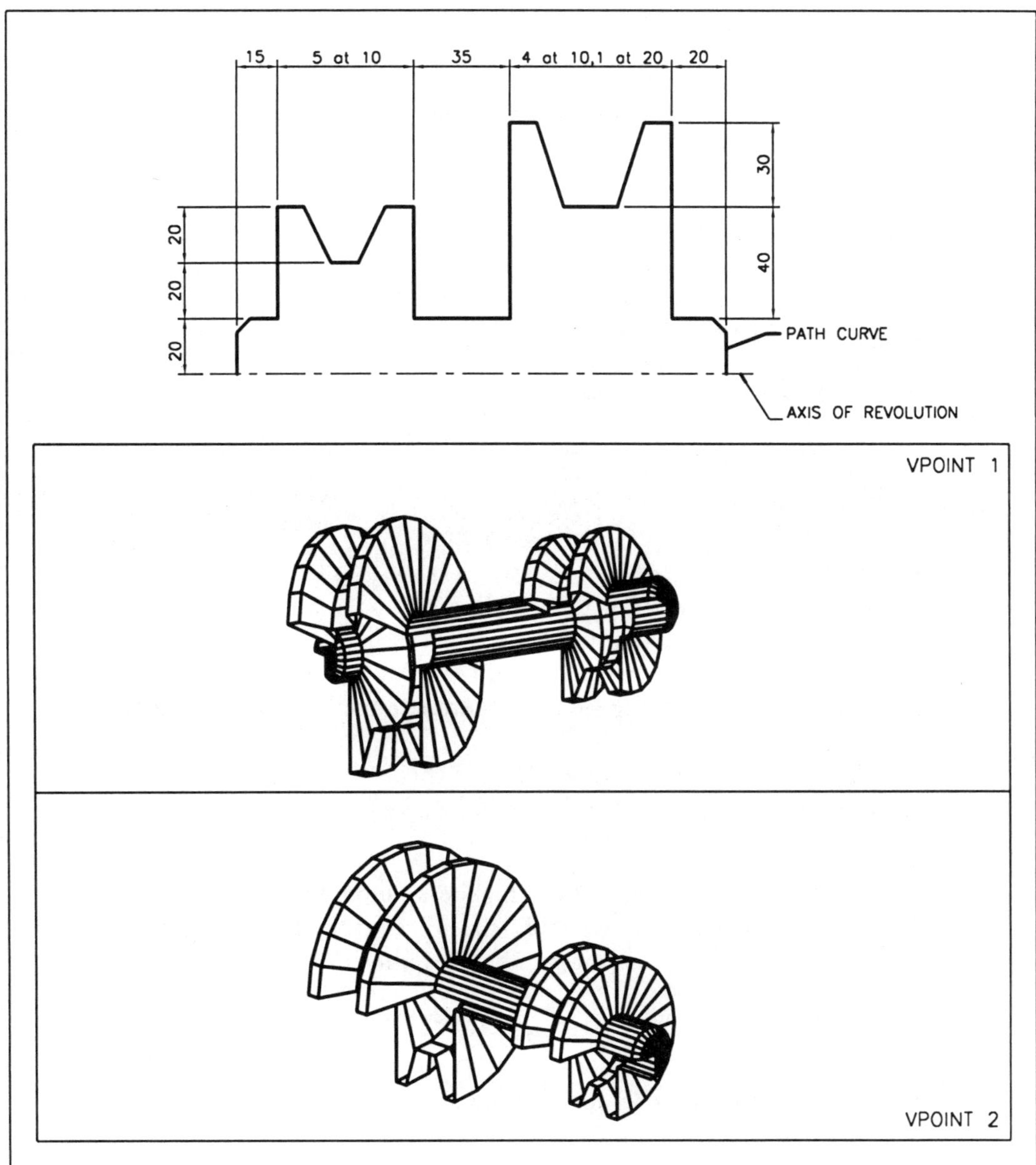
15
5 at 10
35
4 at 10,1 at 20
20
30
40
20
20
20
PATH CURVE
AXIS OF REVOLUTION
VPOINT 1
VPOINT 2

Assignment 49

Topographic contour map

This assignment is quite involved and the various steps have been listed to help with it.

Set up

Begin a new drawing with:

(a) limits (–5, –5) to (65, 45)
(b) set units to decimal with two decimal places
(c) grid 5 and snap to suit
(d) create five new layers:

usage	*name*	*colour*
contours	CONTOUR	magenta
text	TEXT	blue
grid	GRID	red
grid points	GRIDEL	white
elevation	COORD	green

Step 1

1. Set an elevation of 47 with 0 thickness.
2. (a) Draw the 40 × 40 grid.
   (b) Add the coordinate text 0, 10, 20, 30, 40 at height 1.
3. Add the other text (e.g. 46.0, 47.2, etc.) at height 0.9 and at a rotation of 45.
   Note: I used array and DDEDIT for this.
4. Draw in the north and scale symbol.

Step 2

1. Set the elevation to 47 with 0 thickness (should be)
2. Using a closed polyline, draw the 47 contour line using the *x*, *y* coordinate data listed (the numbers are the entry order):

coords		*coords*		*coords*		*coords*	
1	8.33, 0	4	4.71, 30	7	30, 38.26	10	38.57, 10
2	0, 9.33	5	10, 33.6	8	37.04, 30	11	30, 2.5
3	0, 25	6	20, 37.6	9	40, 20	12	25, 0

3. Set the elevation to 48 and thickness to 0.

4. With a 0.15 wide closed polyline, draw the 48 contour line using the following data:

coords	*coords*	*coords*	*coords*
1 20, 6	4 10, 29.47	7 30, 35	10 31.43, 10
2 10, 10	5 11, 30	8 33.33, 30	11 30, 8.75
3 1, 20	6 20, 33.6	9 33.15	

5. With the elevation set to 49 (0 thickness) draw a 0 wide closed polyline using:

coords	*coords*	*coords*
1 10, 15.66	4 20, 29.33	7 30, 15.71
2 6, 20	5 30, 30	8 20, 13.31
3 10, 24.21	6 32.31, 20	

6. Set the elevation to 50 with 0 thickness and draw a 0.15 wide closed polyline with:

coords	*coords*
1 20, 18.89	3 20, 21.54
2 15, 20	4 23.33, 20

Step 3

With polyline edit, use the FIT option and select each polyline contour. Add the contour text.

Step 4

Set a 3D viewpoint.

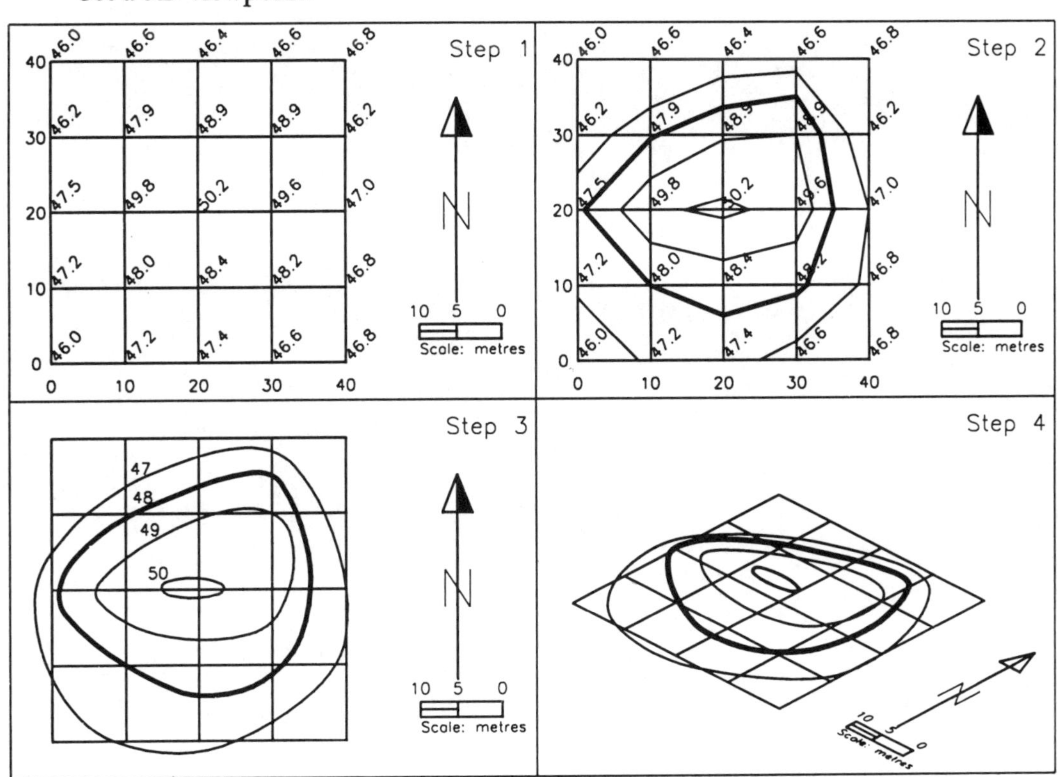

Assignment 50

Metric bolt

Draw the bolt (what sizes?) and complete the table using **three** different text fonts.

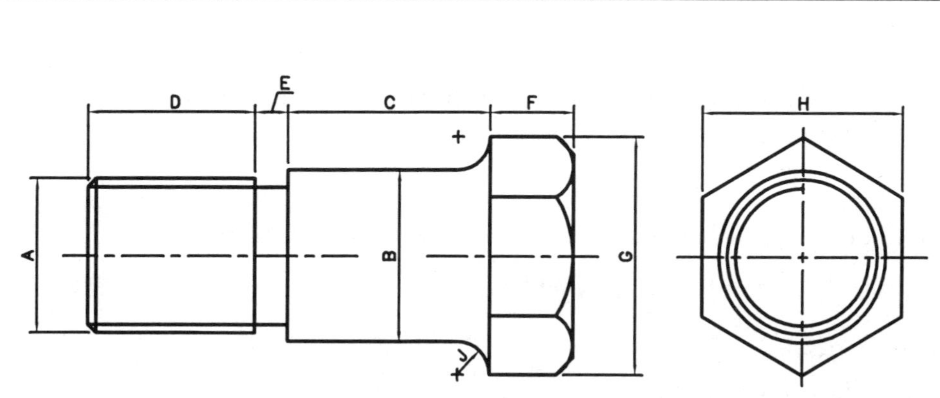

ITEM	A	B	C	D	E	F	G	H	J
1	M6x1	8	10	8	2	4	?	10	2
2	M8x1.25	10	12	10	2	5.5	?	13	2
3	M10x1.5	12	16	12	3	7	?	17	3
4	M12x1.75	16	20	16	3	8	?	19	3
5	M18x2	20	24	20	4	10	?	24	4

Assignment 51

Gasket and flip-flop

Two entirely different exercises which have to be completed on the one A3 sheet.

Gasket
Traditional type of component which requires some tangency.

All the dimensions have to be added.

JK flip-flop
Basically a simple exercise using multiple copy.

The sizes are your own.

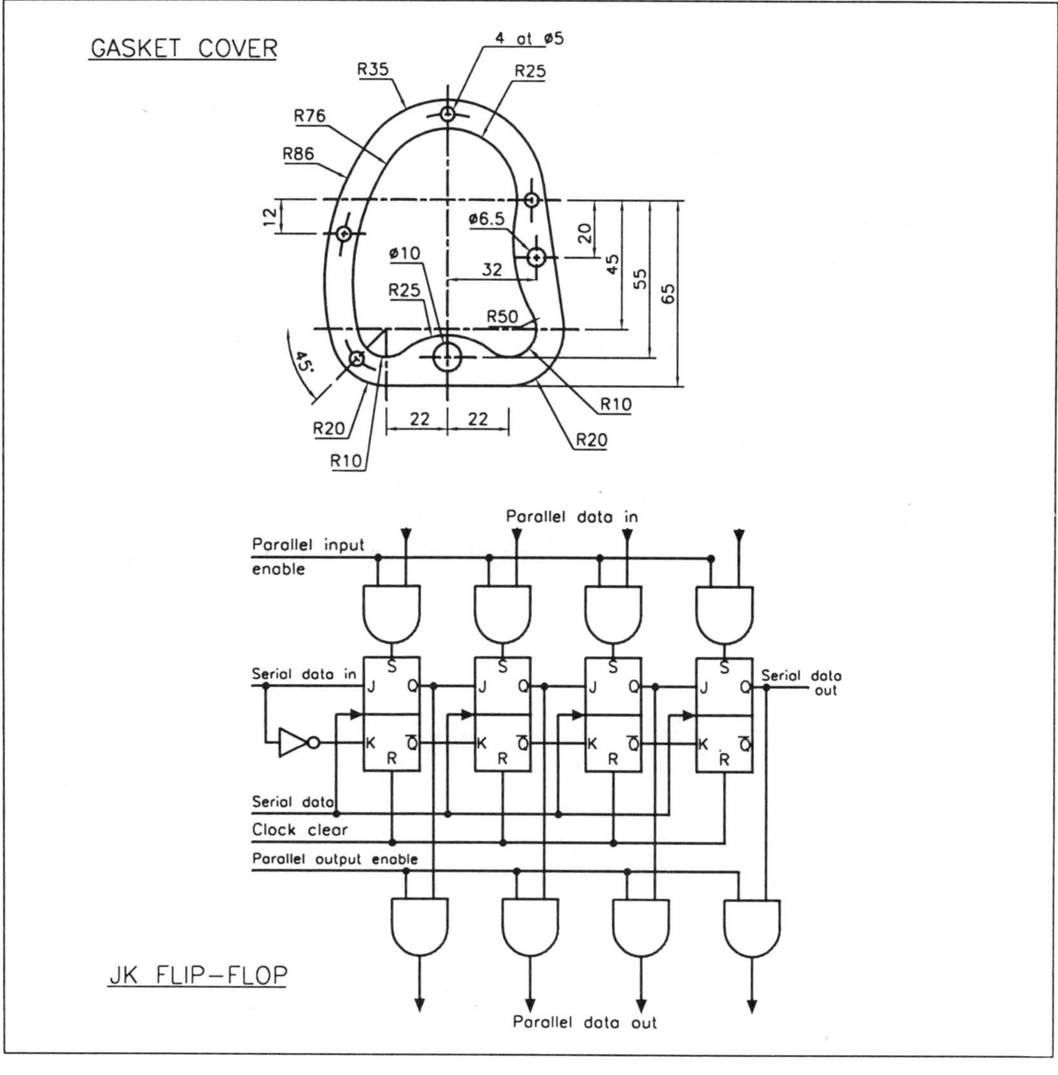
GASKET COVER
4 at ø5
R35
R25
R76
R86
12
ø6.5
20
45
55
65
ø10
32
R25
R50
45°
R10
R20
22
22
R20
R10
Parallel data in
Parallel input
enable
Serial data in
S
J
Q
K
R
Serial data
out
Serial data
Clock clear
Parallel output enable
JK FLIP-FLOP
Parallel data out

Assignment 52

Loci problem

As the crank *OA* rotates, the end *B* of the rod is always constrained to move along the line *PQ*.

For one complete revolution of *OA*, you have to plot the locus of *R* (a point on *AB*) as:

(a) a series of points
(b) a closed polyline

The following values should be used:

OA:	50
AB:	200
AR:	125

Task

Investigate the edit polyline options of FIT and SPLINE on the path curve.

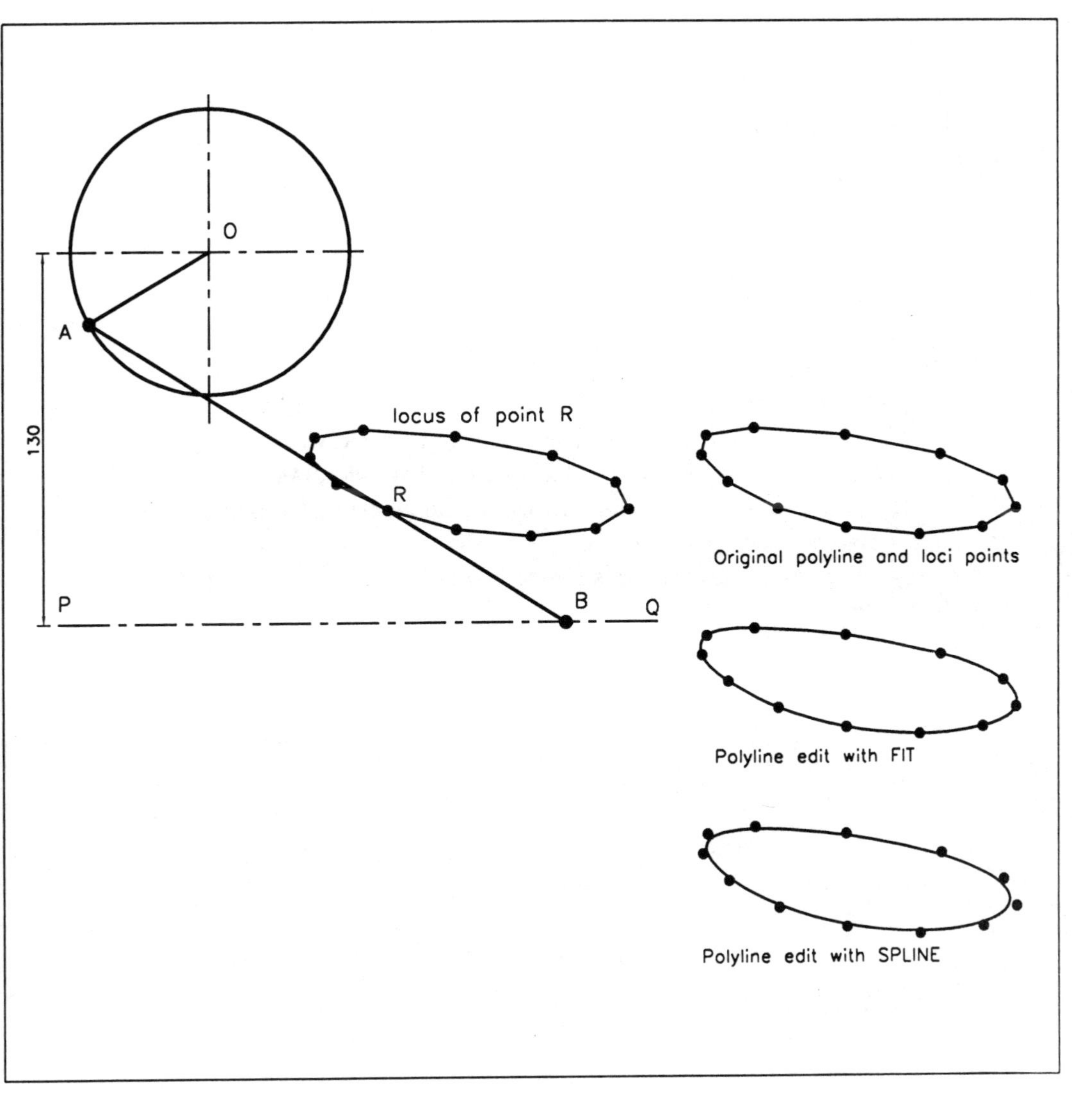
O
A
130
locus of point R
R
P
B
Q
Original polyline and loci points
Polyline edit with FIT
Polyline edit with SPLINE

Assignment 53

Mobile phone

This exercise is in two parts:

1. Draw the two given orthographic views, adding all dimensions.
2. Create a 3D wire-frame model of the component.

Hints

(a) two viewports needed
(b) current layers frozen must be used
(c) wire-frame requires UCS positions to be set and saved
(d) text has to be added to the surface on the keys
(e) the elliptical ear-piece is easier than it would appear
(f) you will need to zoom in on certain parts of the phone – use paper space for this
(g) a bit of perseverance is needed to complete this assignment.

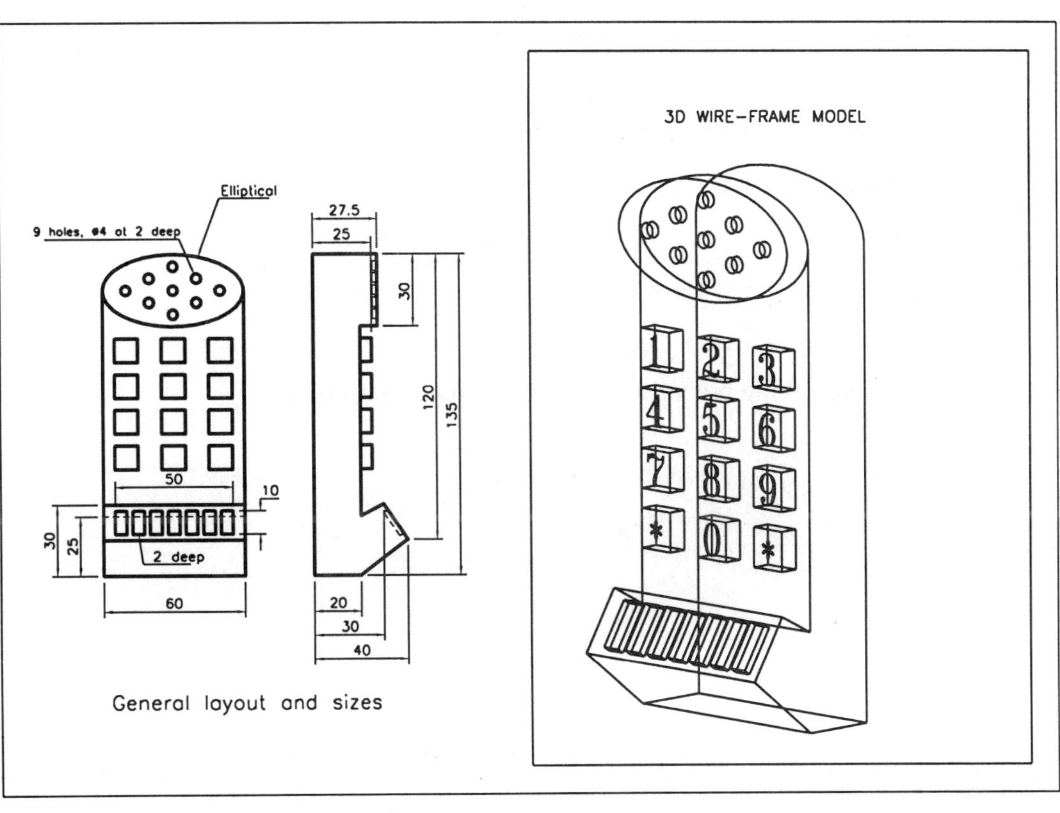

General layout and sizes

Assignment 54

Pets

1. Construct a 10×10 grid and zoom in on it.
2. Set the grid and snap to 2.
3. Draw the two pet symbols, using the grid picture as a guide.
4. Copy the pet symbol to other parts of the screen.
5. Scale as required.
6. Add hatching **but remember hatching can fill disks.**

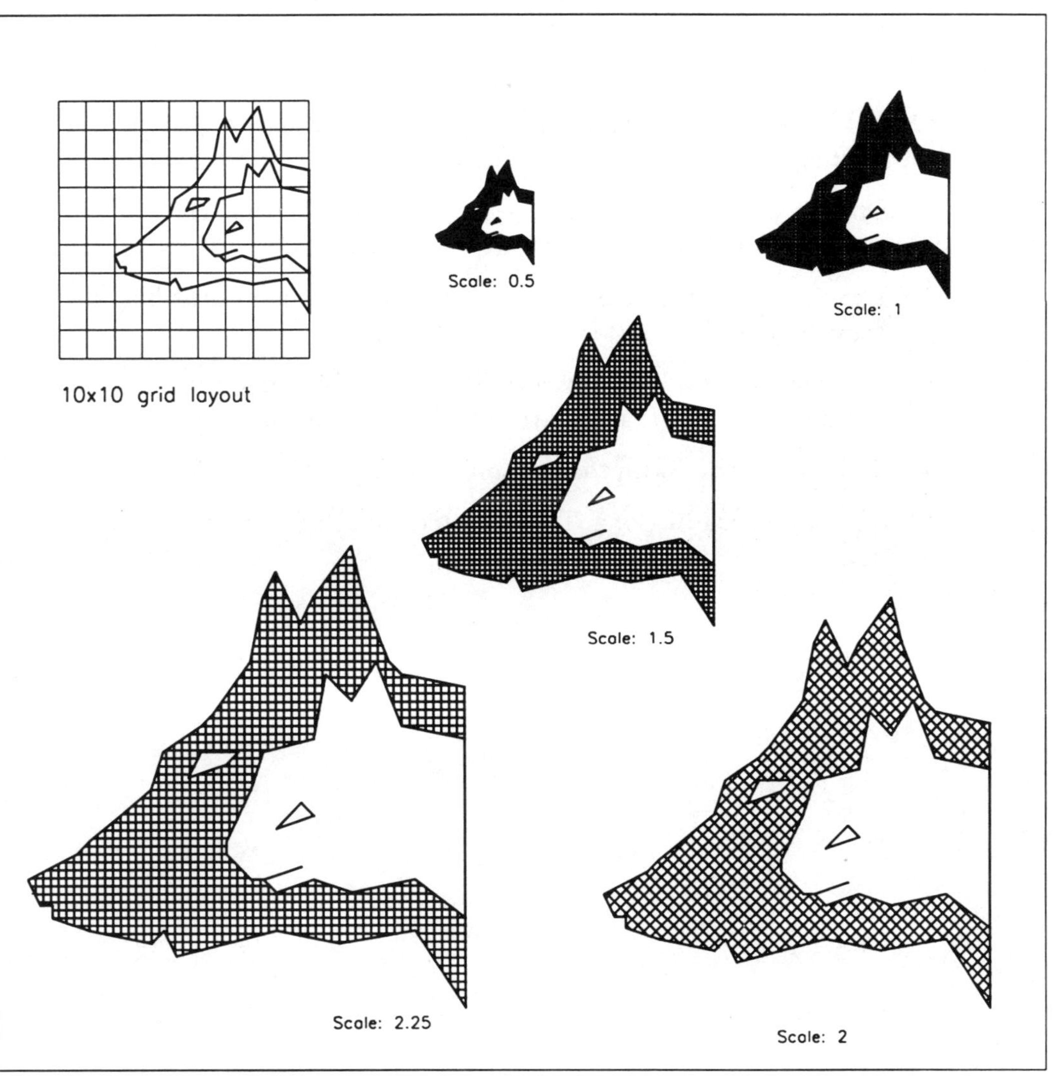
10x10 grid layout
Scale: 0.5
Scale: 1
Scale: 1.5
Scale: 2.25
Scale: 2

Assignment 55

Illusions 1

Optical illusions can be created with CAD, and the following are five of the most common.

1. Draw two horizontal lines of length 60 and 40 apart. The inclined lines are all at 45 degrees. The snap on helps.
2. Two vertical lines of length 60 and 100 apart. The inclined lines are drawn in to suit.
3. The two circles *X* and *Y* have a diameter of 20. Draw a larger circle and array it about *X*, and draw a smaller circle and array it about *Y*.
4. Easy to construct with the grid and snap. The 'tread' is 20.
5. AB and BC are 100 long. The three rectangular boxes are 40 × 20 in size.

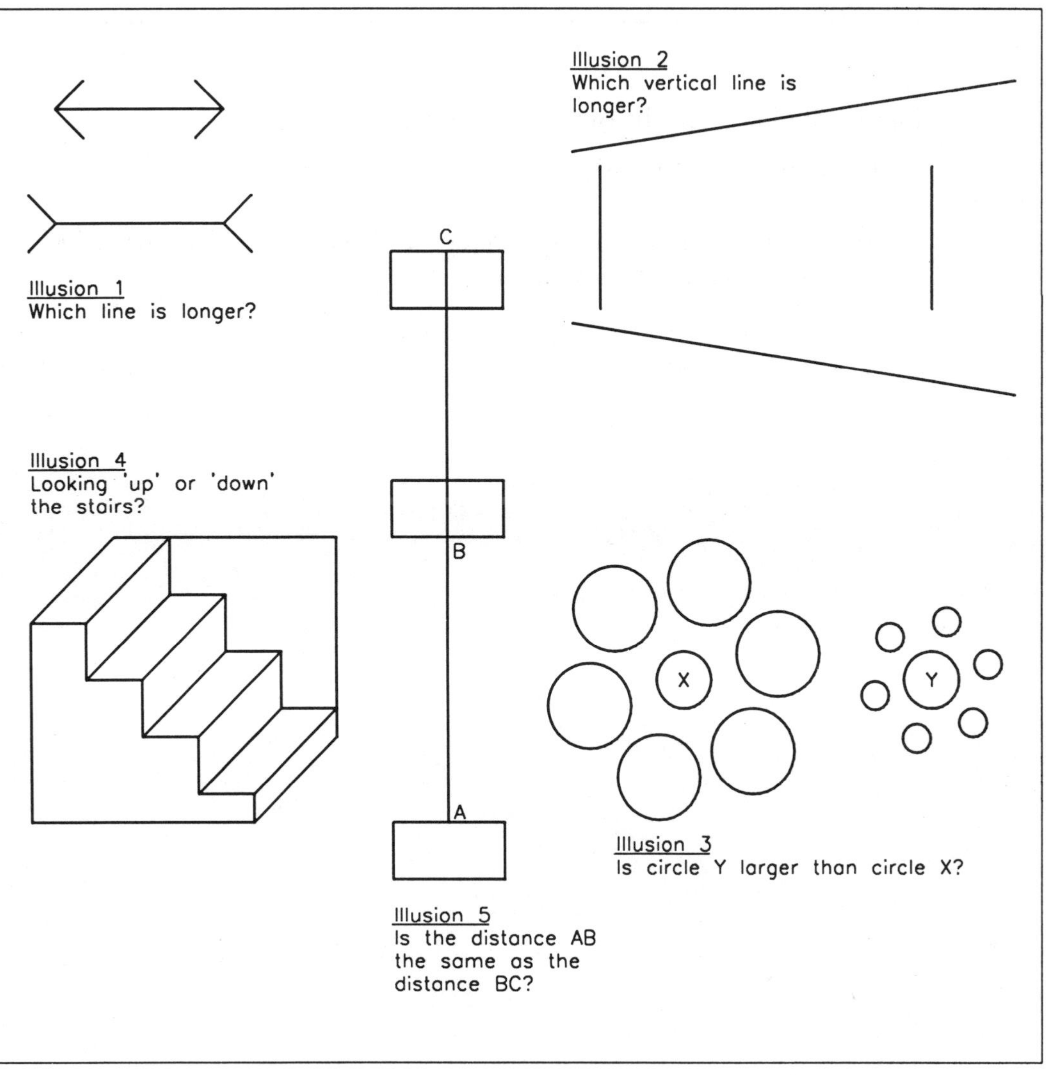
Illusion 2
Which vertical line is longer?
C
Illusion 1
Which line is longer?
Illusion 4
Looking 'up' or 'down' the stairs?
B
X
Y
A
Illusion 3
Is circle Y larger than circle X?
Illusion 5
Is the distance AB the same as the distance BC?

Assignment 56

Dimensions

Draw and dimension the two components.

The 'tolerance sizes' can be:

(a) added as new dimensions styles
(b) added by altering the appropriate DIMVAR at the keyboard, i.e. dimtp, dimtm, dimtol, dimlim, etc.

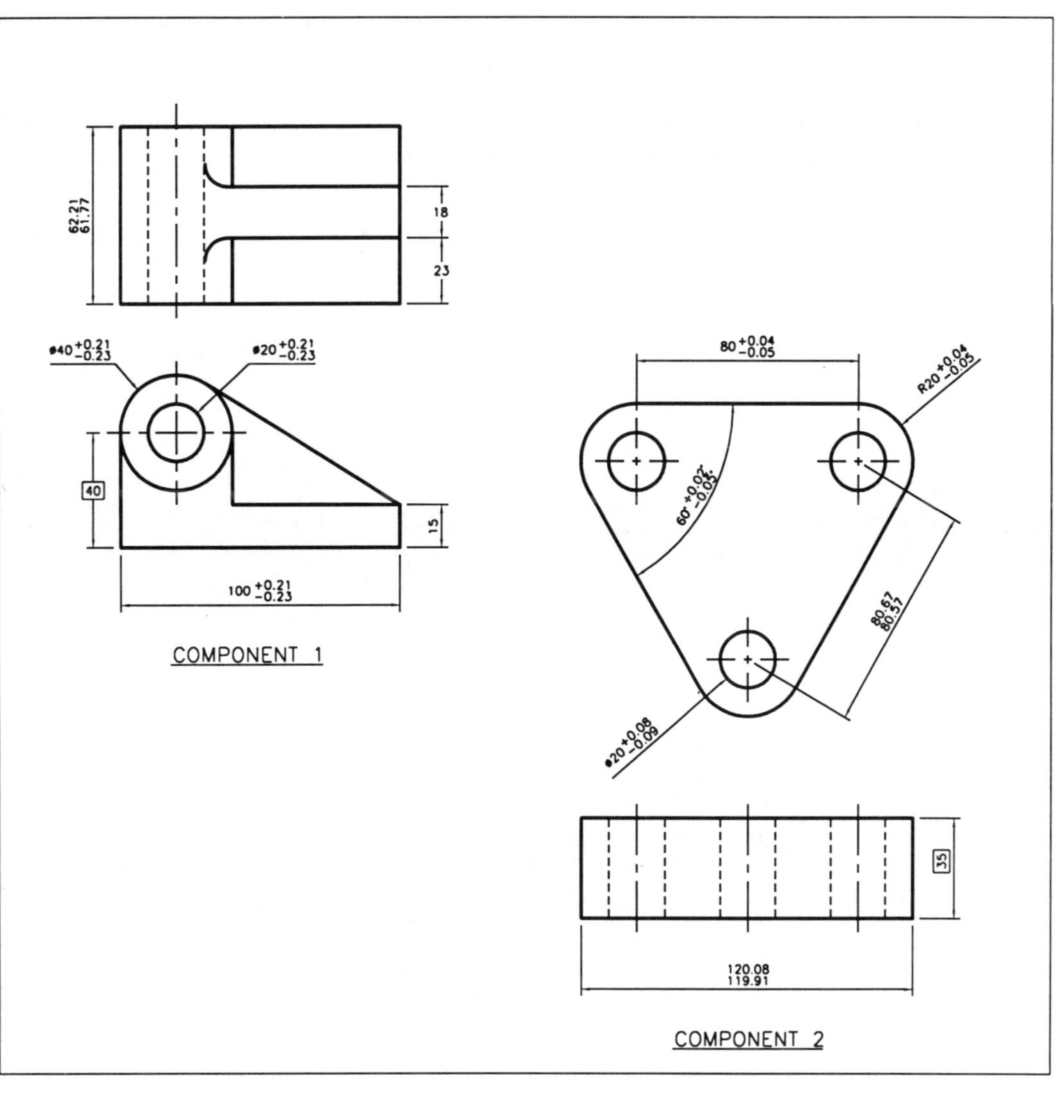
62.21
61.77
18
23
ø40 +0.21 −0.23
ø20 +0.21 −0.23
40
15
100 +0.21 −0.23
COMPONENT 1
80 +0.04 −0.05
R20 +0.04 −0.05
60° +0.02° −0.03°
80.67
80.57
ø20 +0.08 −0.09
35
120.08
119.91
COMPONENT 2

Assignment 57

Seating plugs

Two components to be drawn and dimensioned, both involving 'half-sections'. Adding the dimensions takes some time.

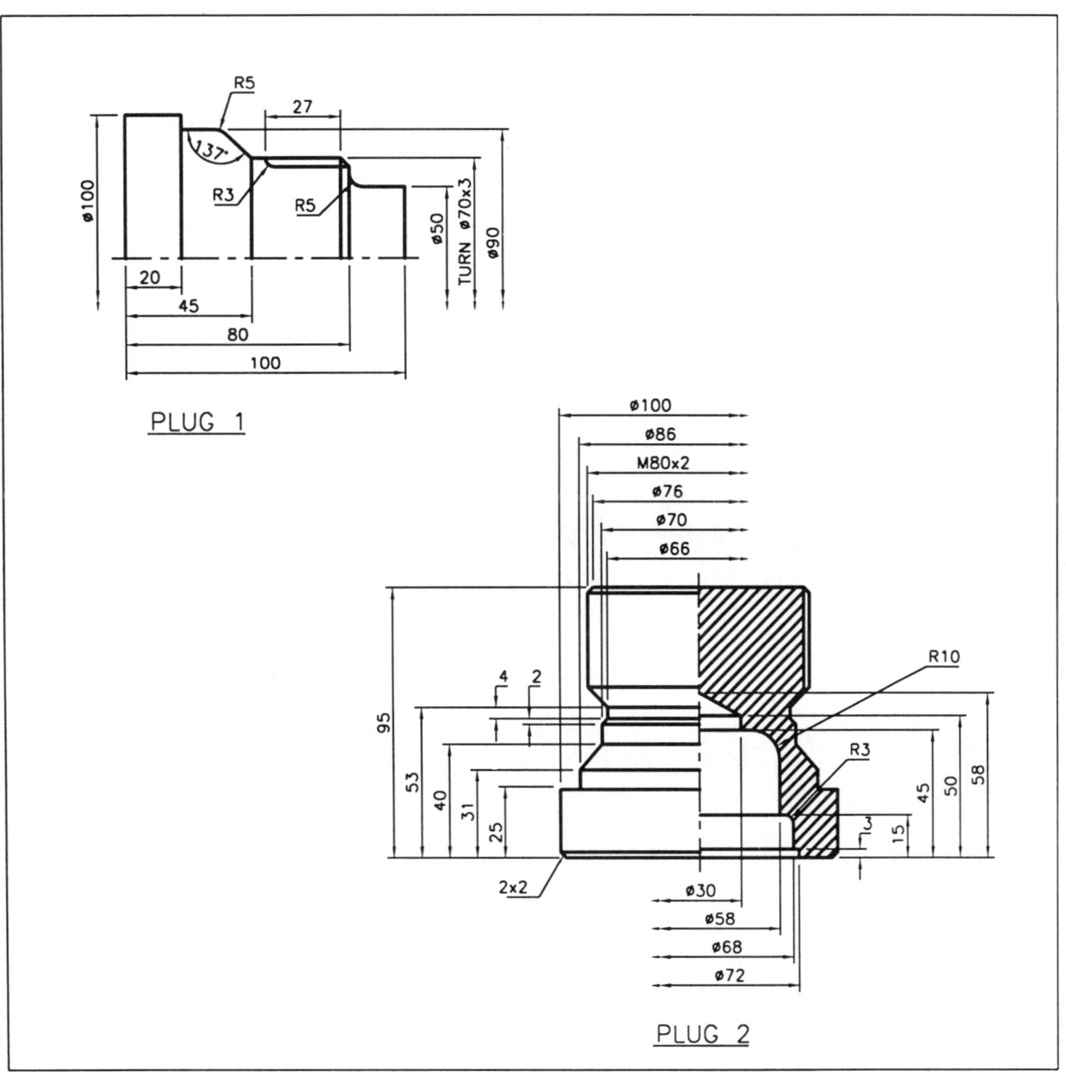
R5
27
137°
R3
R5
ø100
ø50
TURN ø70x3
ø90
20
45
80
100
PLUG 1
ø100
ø86
M80x2
ø76
ø70
ø66
R10
4
2
95
53
40
31
25
R3
45
50
58
3
15
2x2
ø30
ø58
ø68
ø72
PLUG 2

Assignment 58

Bypass plate

A relatively straightforward component to be drawn and dimensioned.

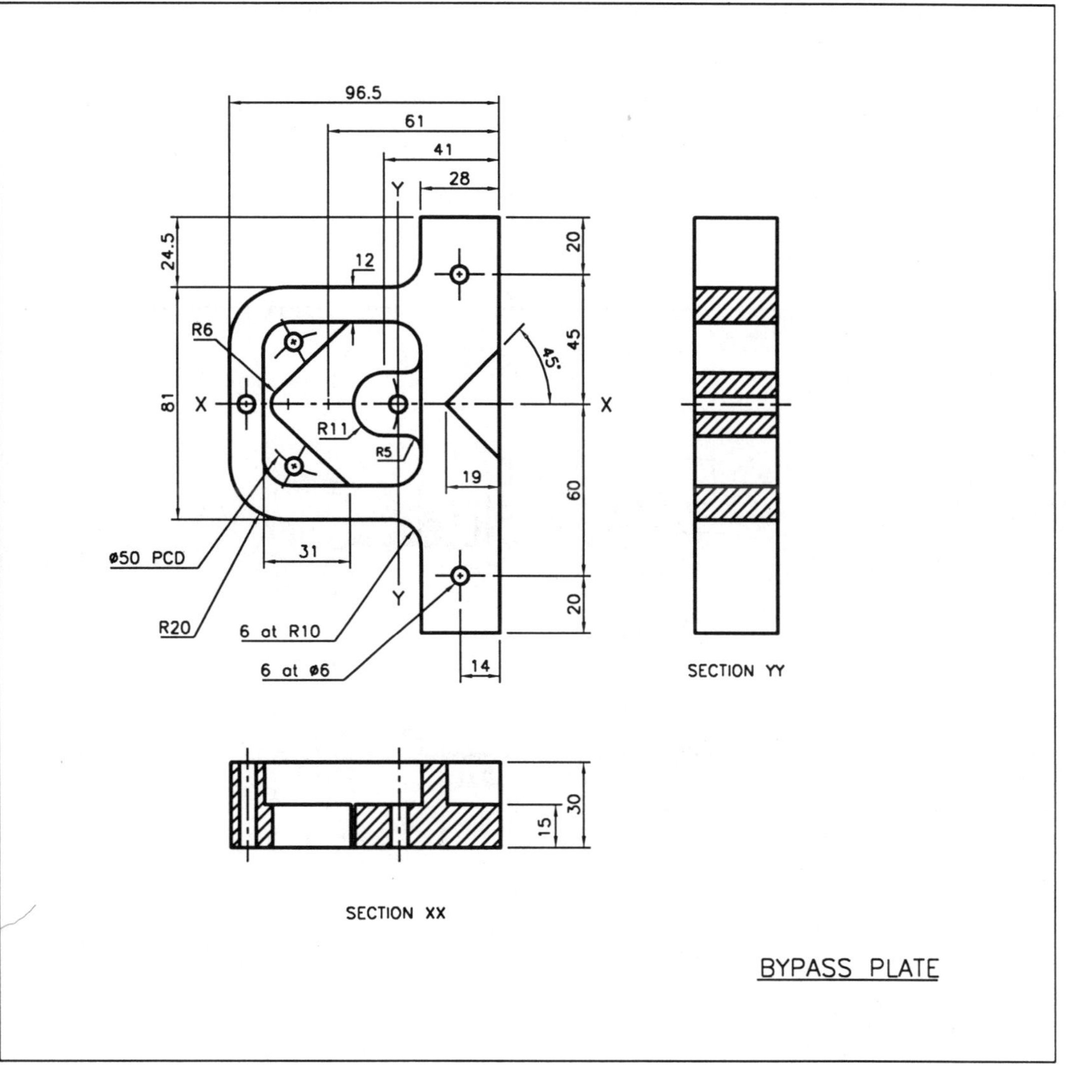
96.5
61
41
28
Y
24.5
12
20
45
45°
R6
81
X
X
R11
R5
19
60
ø50 PCD
31
Y
20
R20
6 at R10
6 at ø6
14
SECTION YY
30
15
SECTION XX
BYPASS PLATE

Assignment 59

Electrical circuit

1. Create the nine blocks using the sizes and names below, using your discretion as appropriate.
2. Insert the blocks at 0.5 scale, and complete the circuit diagram.
3. Add all text.

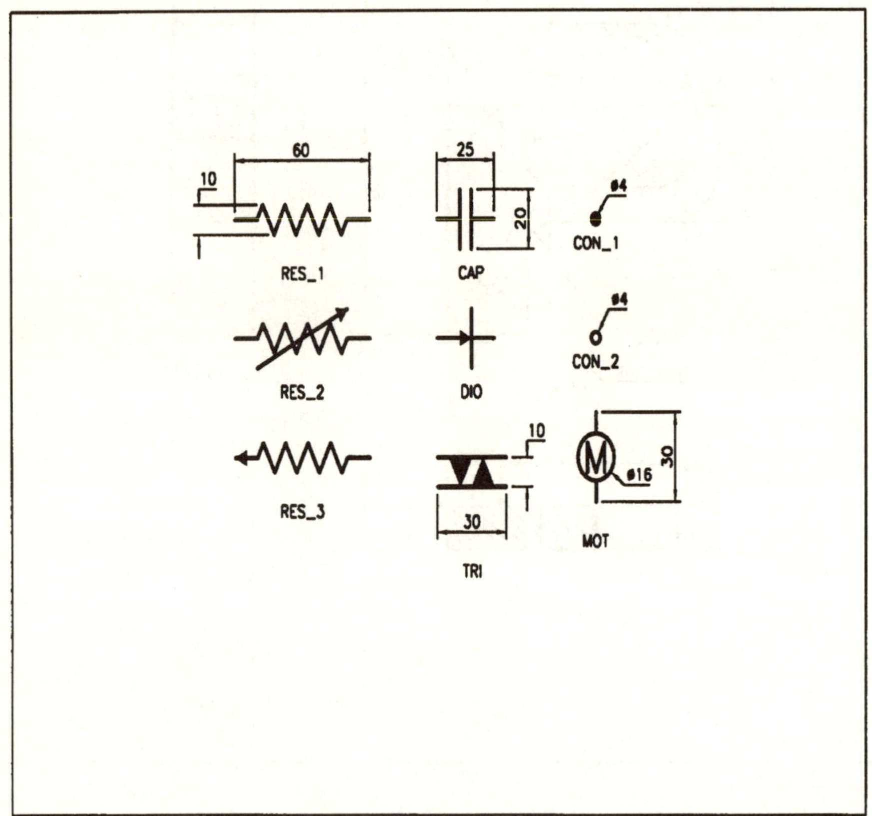

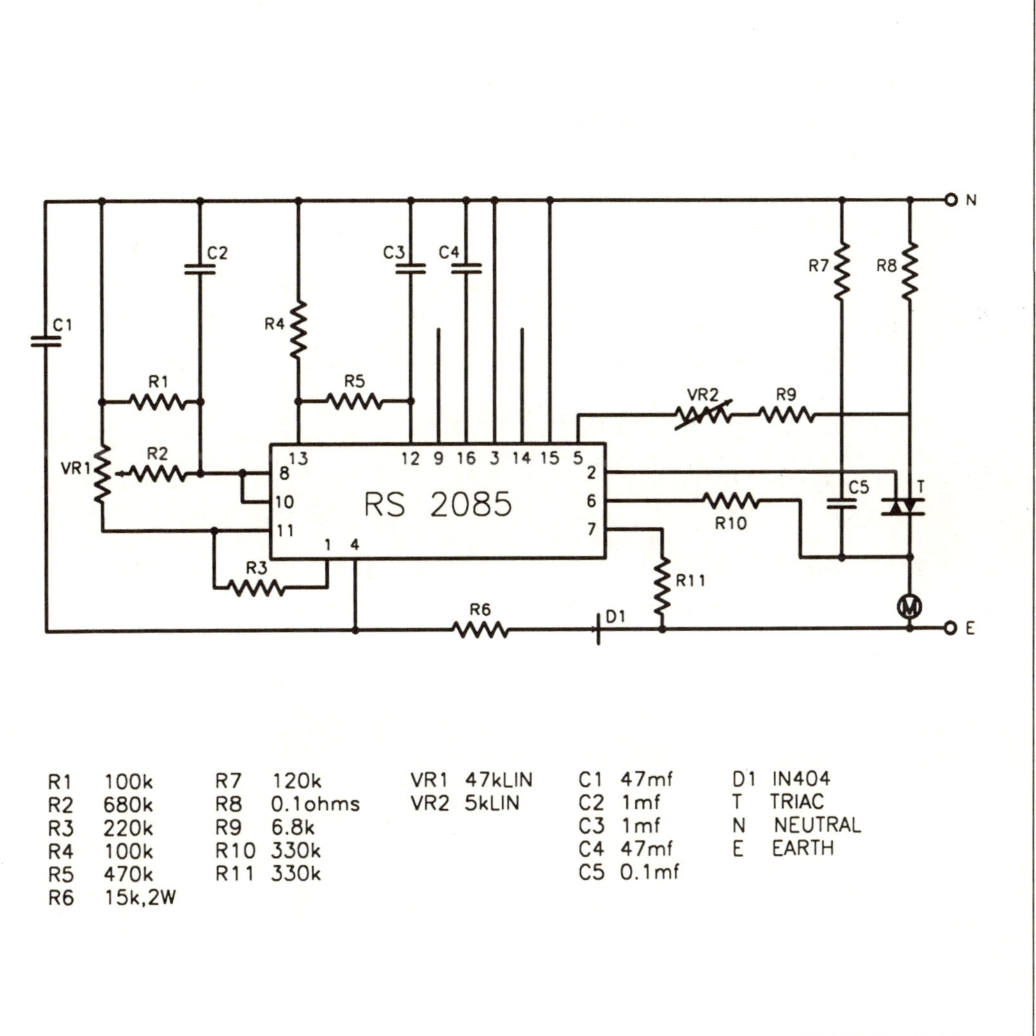
N
E
C1
C2
C3
C4
C5
R1
R2
R3
R4
R5
R6
R7
R8
R9
R10
R11
VR1
VR2
D1
T
M
RS 2085
13
12 9 16 3 14 15 5
8
10
11
1 4
2
6
7
R1 100k
R2 680k
R3 220k
R4 100k
R5 470k
R6 15k,2W
R7 120k
R8 0.1ohms
R9 6.8k
R10 330k
R11 330k
VR1 47kLIN
VR2 5kLIN
C1 47mf
C2 1mf
C3 1mf
C4 47mf
C5 0.1mf
D1 IN404
T TRIAC
N NEUTRAL
E EARTH

Assignment 60

Wire-frame house with hatched roof

Create the wire-frame model of the house in a four viewport (paper-space) configuration to display:

(a) a 3D view with dimensions added
(b) a 3D view with all hatching added to the roof
(c) a front view
(d) a top view

Note

1. Currently freeze certain layers for dimensions and hatching.
2. Take care with the hatch scale. I used:
   Pattern: BRICK
   Scale: 20
   Angle: 0
3. I created four new hatch layers for the roof, and have displayed the house with certain of these layers currently frozen.
4. Remember to centre the model in the viewports.

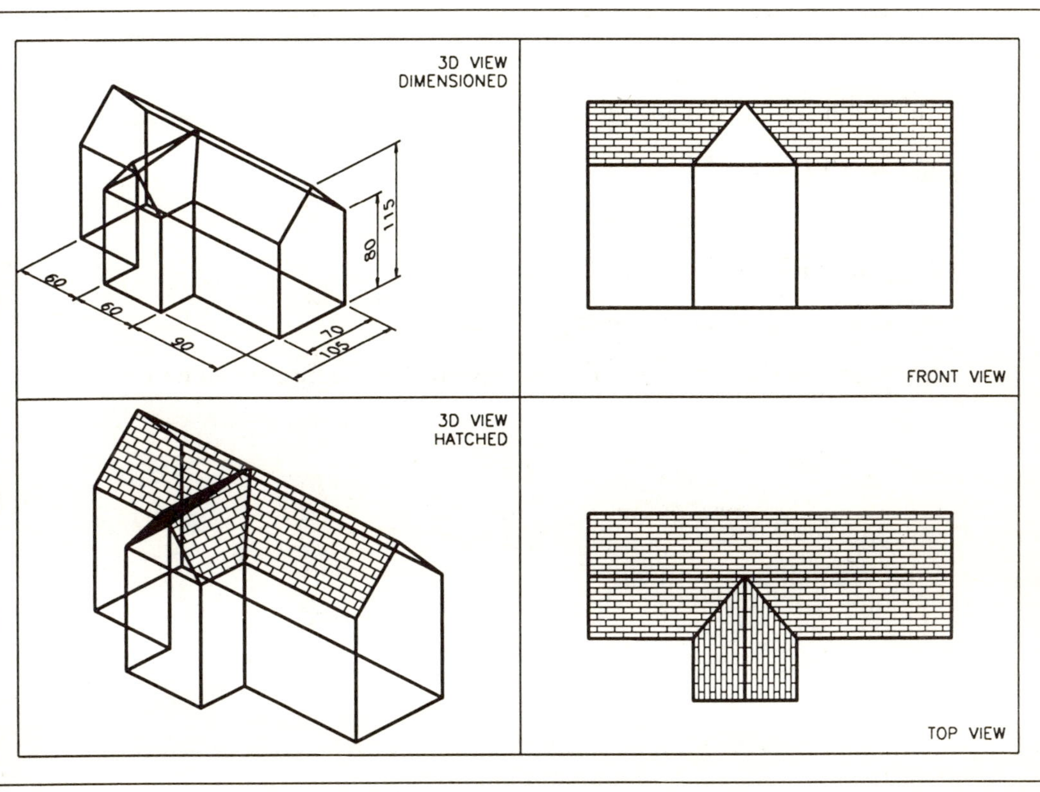
3D VIEW
DIMENSIONED
60
60
90
70
105
80
115
FRONT VIEW
3D VIEW
HATCHED
TOP VIEW

Assignment 61

House plan

Draw, dimension and add all text with:

1. Set to a scale of 1:50 for A3 paper.
2. Grid: 500, Snap: 250.
3. Wall thickness, exterior: 250, interior: 100.
4. Doors and windows are at your discretion.
5. Suppress the dimension line extensions for the internal dimensions.

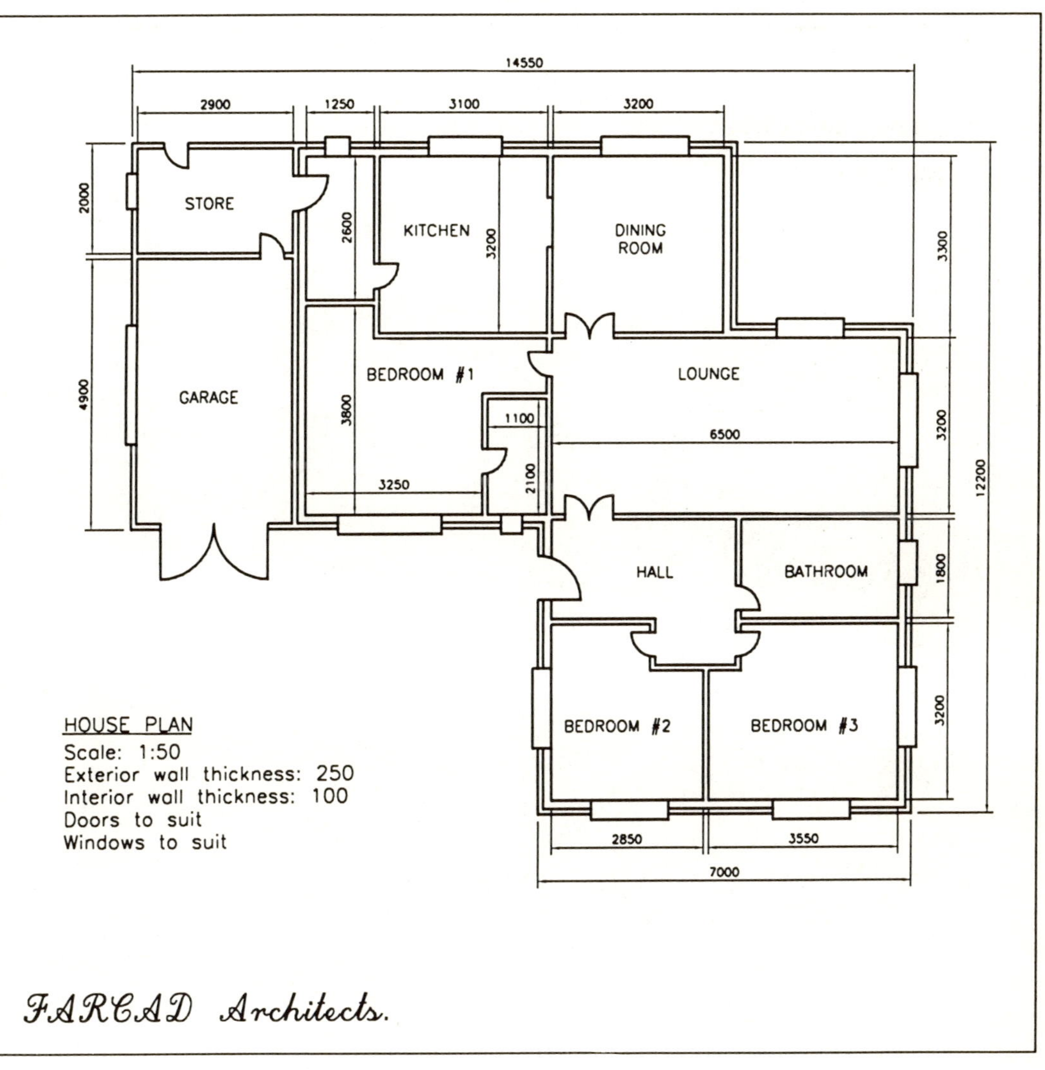

14550
2900
1250
3100
3200
2000
STORE
2600
KITCHEN
3200
DINING
ROOM
3300
4900
GARAGE
BEDROOM #1
3800
1100
2100
3250
LOUNGE
6500
3200
12200
HALL
BATHROOM
1800
BEDROOM #2
BEDROOM #3
3200
2850
3550
7000
HOUSE PLAN
Scale: 1:50
Exterior wall thickness: 250
Interior wall thickness: 100
Doors to suit
Windows to suit
FARCAD Architects.

Assignment 62

House front

Draw a house front similar to that shown.

No help!

Assignment 63

Have a break

Assignment title says it all.

A coffee and a Kit-Kat?

McFA
REMO

Assignment 64

Light centre designs

Create some light centres using a 100 diameter circle.

Assignment 65

Bearing plate

Draw and fully dimension the sectioned component.

The stepped section lines are different for a bit of variety.

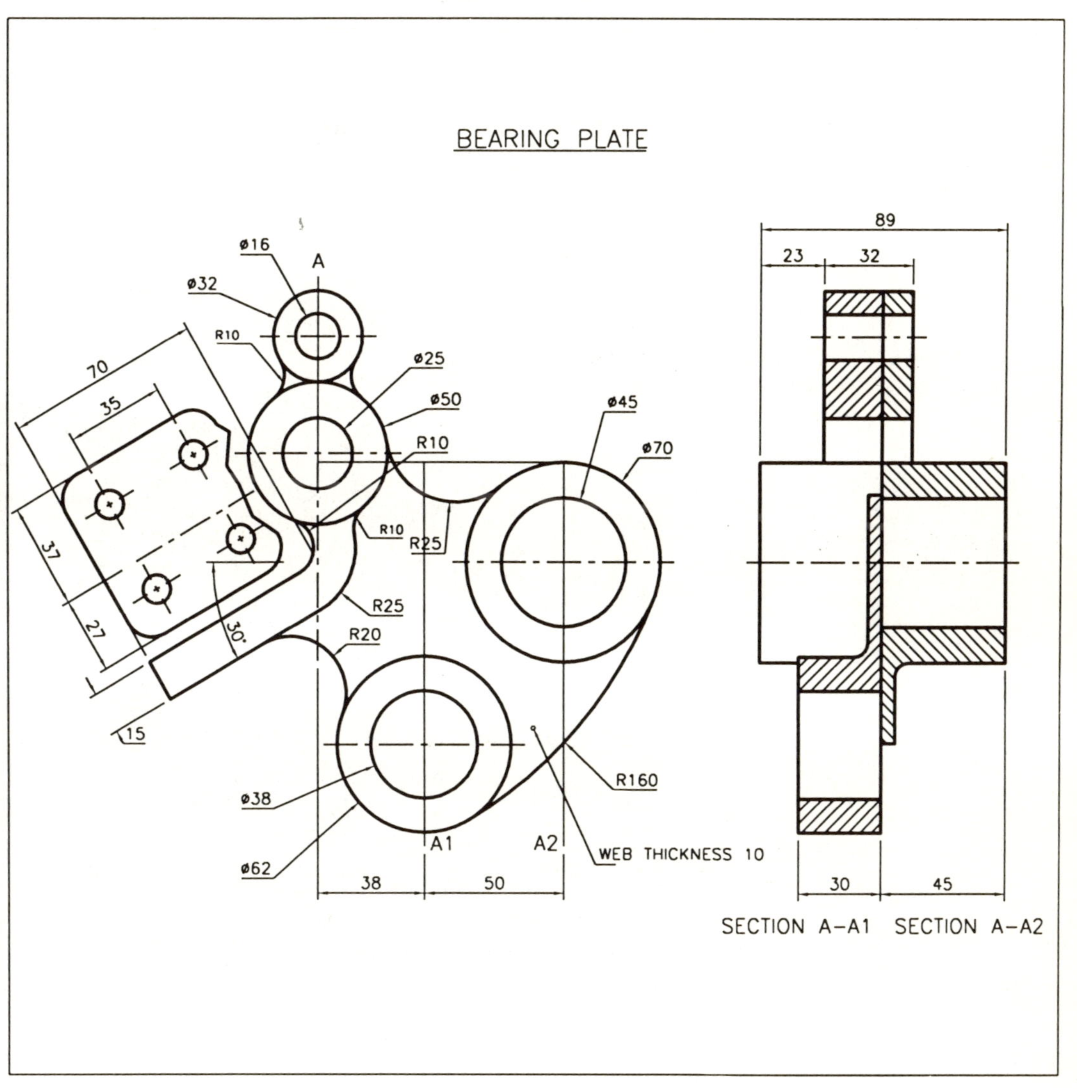
BEARING PLATE
ø16
A
ø32
R10
70
35
ø25
ø50
R10
ø45
ø70
89
23
32
R10
R25
37
R25
27
30°
R20
15
ø38
R160
ø62
A1
A2
WEB THICKNESS 10
38
50
30
45
SECTION A–A1
SECTION A–A2

Assignment 66

Stop link

Component to be drawn sectioned and dimensioned.

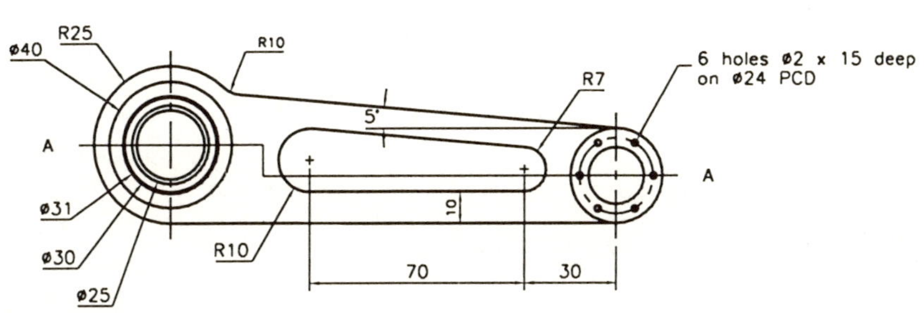

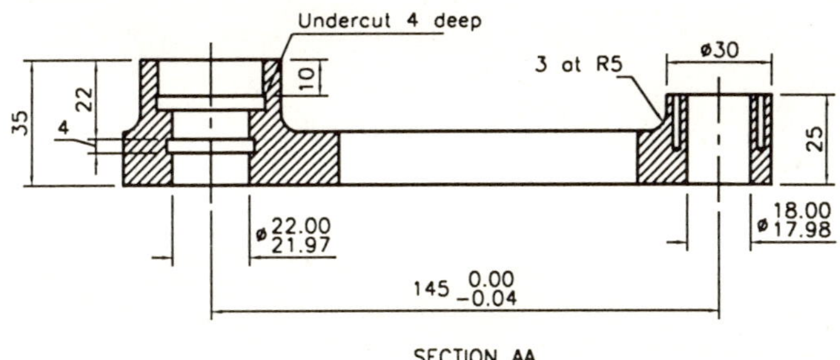

SECTION AA

INFORMATION
Part name: STOP LINK
Scale: 1:1
Date of Issue: 1/4/87
Material: DURALUMIN
Part No: FG12/g34-5C

Assignment 67

Stub axle

Traditional type of drawing but introduces the 'partial section' detail.

Dimensioning is not as easy as it would appear!

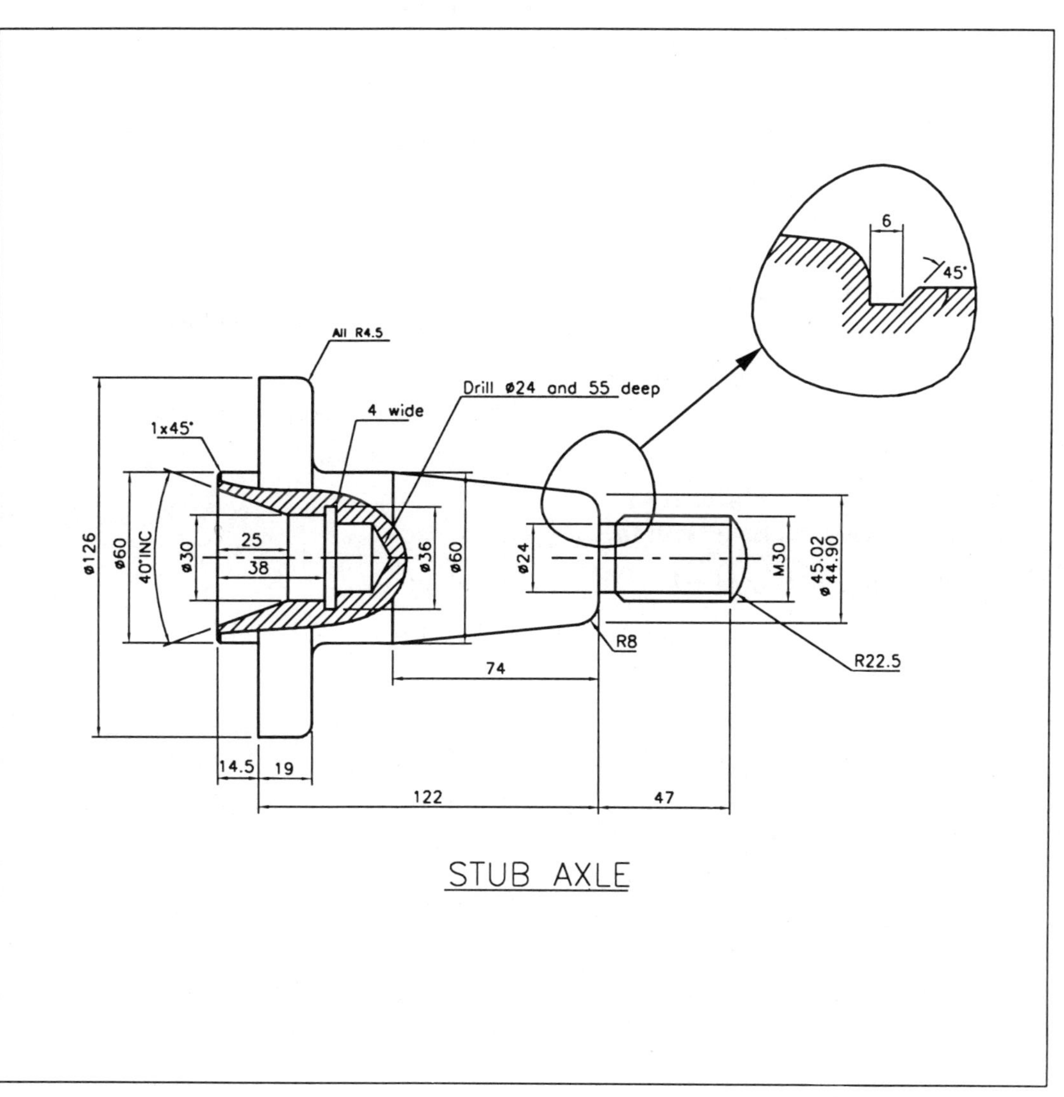
All R4.5
Drill ø24 and 55 deep
4 wide
1x45°
6
45°
ø126
ø60
40°INC
ø30
25
38
ø36
ø60
ø24
M30
ø 45.02
44.90
R8
R22.5
74
14.5
19
122
47
STUB AXLE

Assignment 68

Illusions 2

Four more illusions for you to create and amaze your friends.

6. The white triangle mystery.
   (a) draw two equilateral triangles
   (b) add three donuts to suit
   (c) trim and erase
   (d) can be scaled. The larger the drawing, the better the illusion.
7. Is the letter an S or an H?
   Draw a polyline S, then use the divide-block option to add a saved H block.
8. Impossible object 1
   Draw in oblique with the snap on.
9. Impossible object 2.

   An isometric drawing is required and takes some thought!

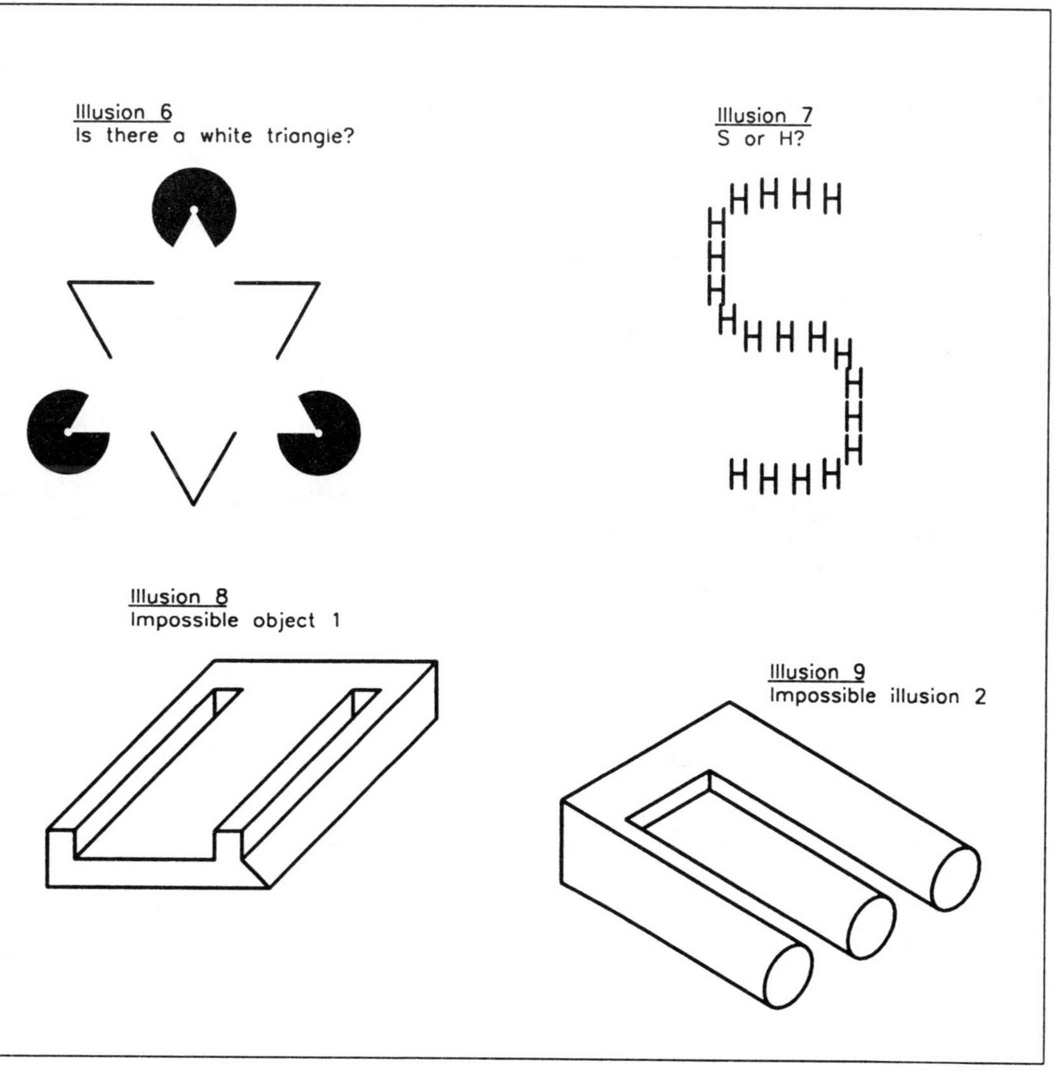
Illusion 6
Is there a white triangle?
Illusion 7
S or H?
Illusion 8
Impossible object 1
Illusion 9
Impossible illusion 2

Assignment 69

Printed circuit board

The partial printed circuit board has to be drawn and all text added.

This is relatively easy but the layout can be tricky, especially as no sizes are given.

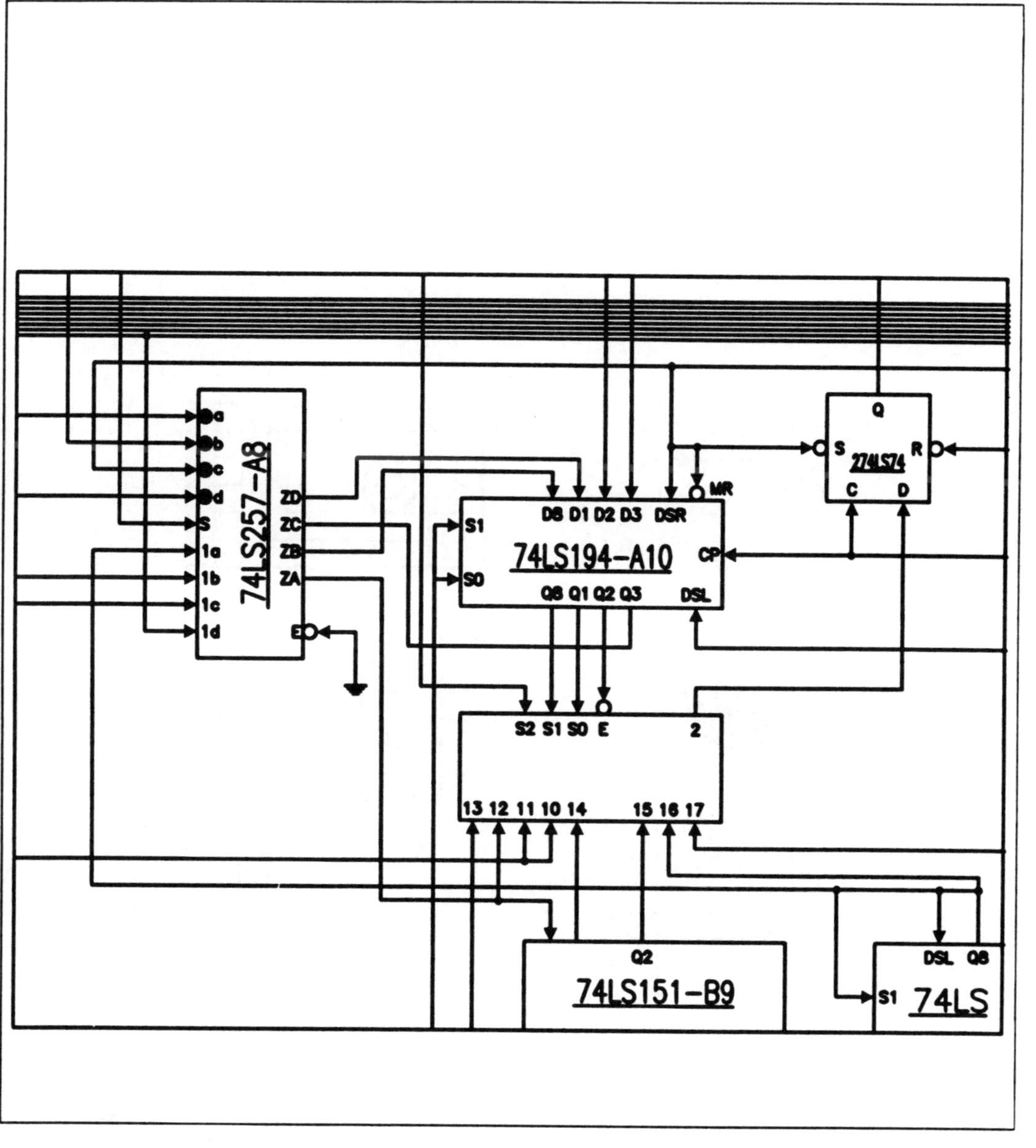
a
b
c
d
S
1a
1b
1c
1d
ZD
ZC
ZB
ZA
E
74LS257-A8
D0 D1 D2 D3 DSR
MR
S1
S0
74LS194-A10
CP
Q0 Q1 Q2 Q3
DSL
Q
S
274LS74
R
C
D
S2 S1 S0 E
2
13 12 11 10 14
15 16 17
Q2
74LS151-B9
DSL Q0
S1
74LS

Assignment 70

Designer garden

1. Set grid to 10 and snap to 5.
2. Create the six garden objects below, using the grid points as reference.
3. Block each object using the given name. The insertion point is at your discretion.
4. Insert each block, and create your own designer garden.

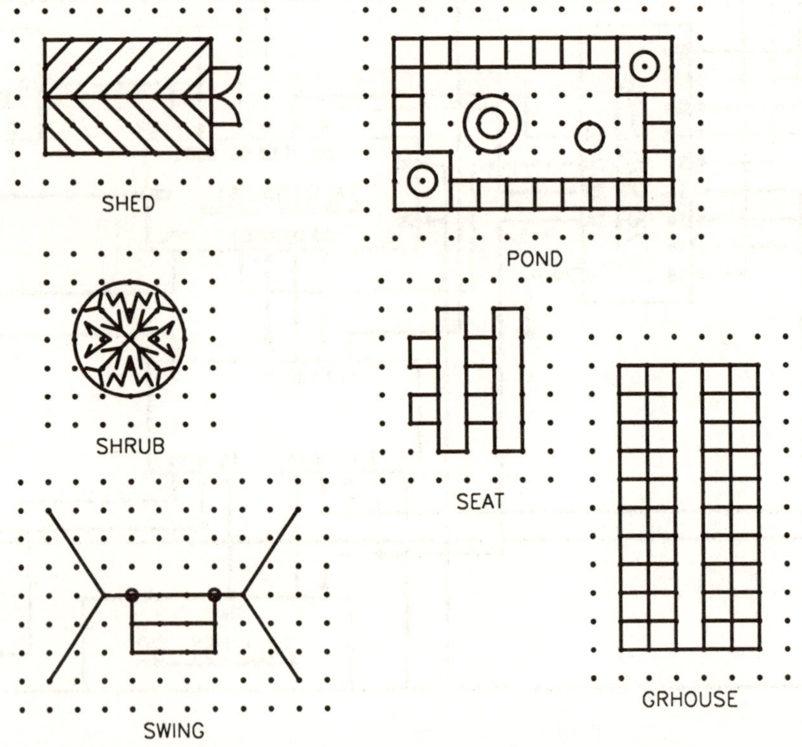

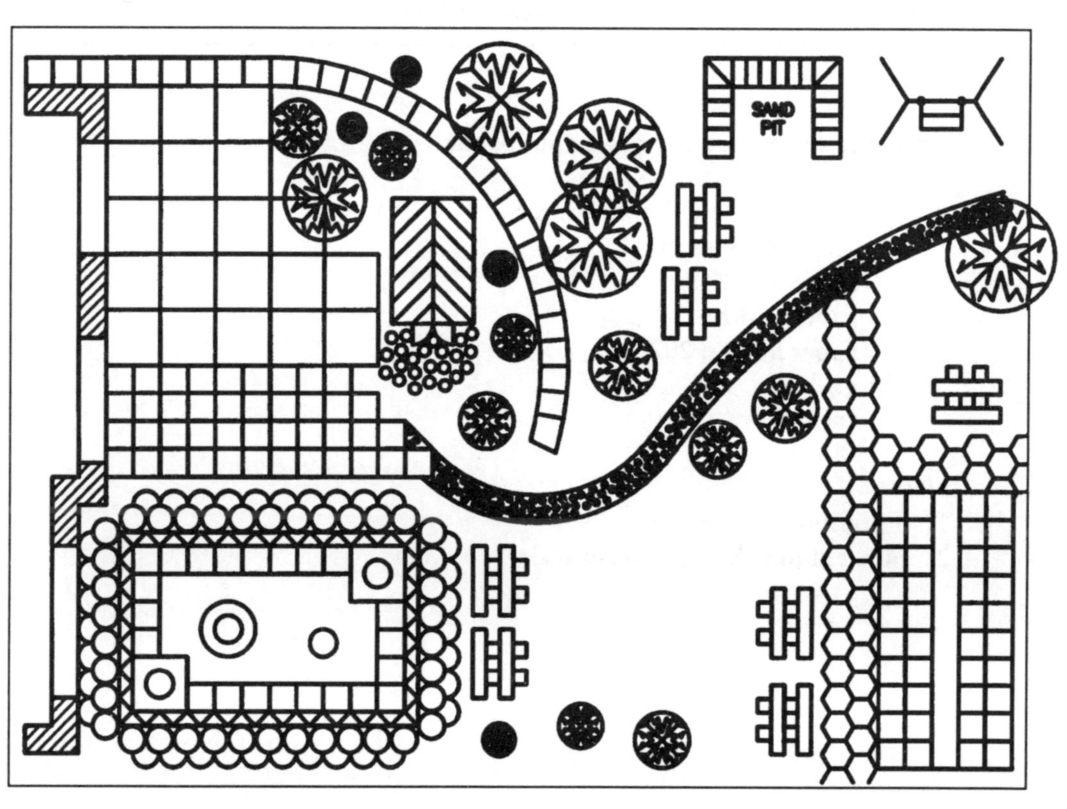
SAND
PIT

Assignment 71

Scaled flat

Draw and dimension the flat layout using:

(a) The **MVSETUP** command with:
units: Architectural
scale: 6″=1′
paper width: 297
paper height: 207

(b) grid: 1′
snap: 6″

Note

1. Enter units as 2′6″, etc.
2. What about the dimension scale?

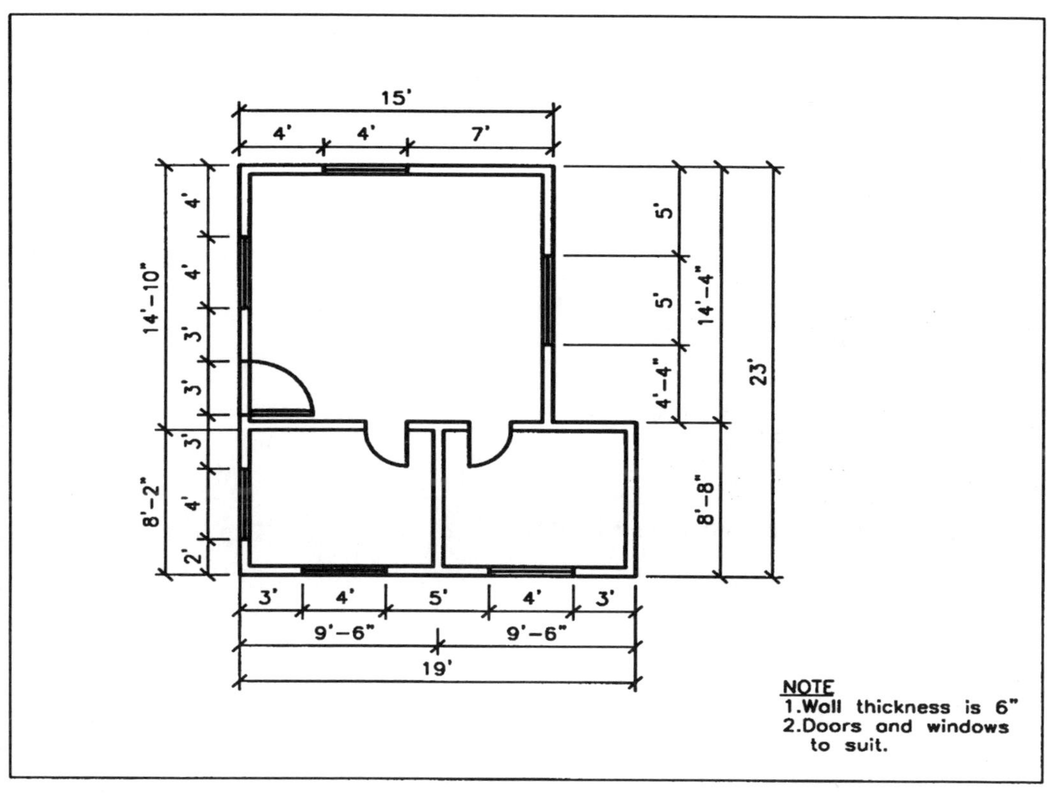
15'
4'
4'
7'
14'-10"
4'
4'
3'
3'
3'
8'-2"
4'
2'
5'
5'
4'-4"
14'-4"
23'
8'-8"
3'
4'
5'
4'
3'
9'-6"
9'-6"
19'
NOTE
1.Wall thickness is 6"
2.Doors and windows
to suit.

Assignment 72

Wall end

Draw, dimension and add all text to the wall end detail.

1. Use MVSETUP with:
   (a) Architectural
   (b) Full
   (c) Width: 297
   (d) Height: 207
2. The hatching used was:
   (a) AR_CONC, scale: 0.5″
   (b) EARTH, scale: 9″
   (c) INSUL, scale: 6″
3. Text size and dimscale value?

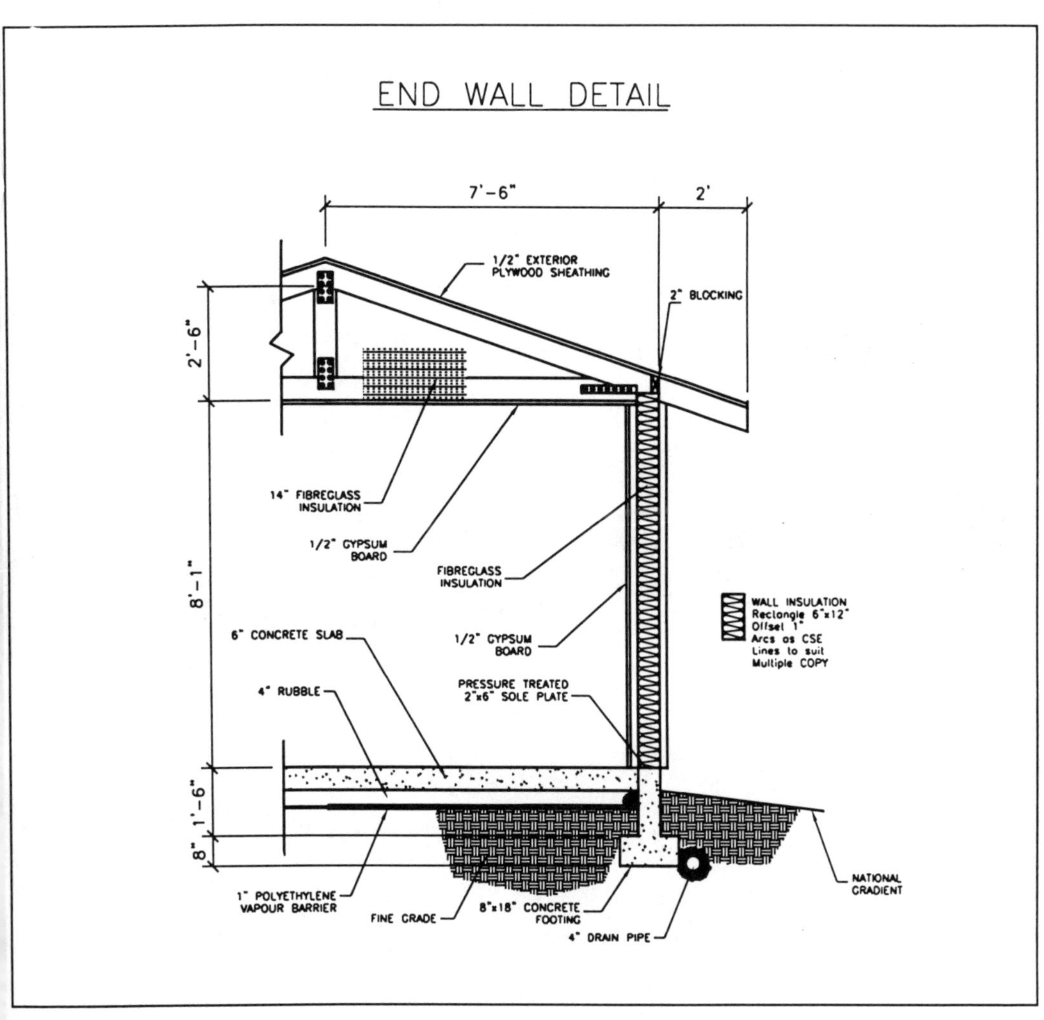
END WALL DETAIL
7'-6"
2'
1/2" EXTERIOR PLYWOOD SHEATHING
2" BLOCKING
2'-6"
14" FIBREGLASS INSULATION
1/2" GYPSUM BOARD
FIBREGLASS INSULATION
8'-1"
WALL INSULATION
Rectangle 6"x12"
Offset 1"
Arcs as CSE
Lines to suit
Multiple COPY
6" CONCRETE SLAB
1/2" GYPSUM BOARD
4" RUBBLE
PRESSURE TREATED 2"x6" SOLE PLATE
1'-6"
8"
NATIONAL GRADIENT
1" POLYETHYLENE VAPOUR BARRIER
FINE GRADE
8"x18" CONCRETE FOOTING
4" DRAIN PIPE

Assignment 73

Pulley assembly

Draw full size the given assembly, adding all hatching.

The sizes are really only for reference.

Note: hatch scales?

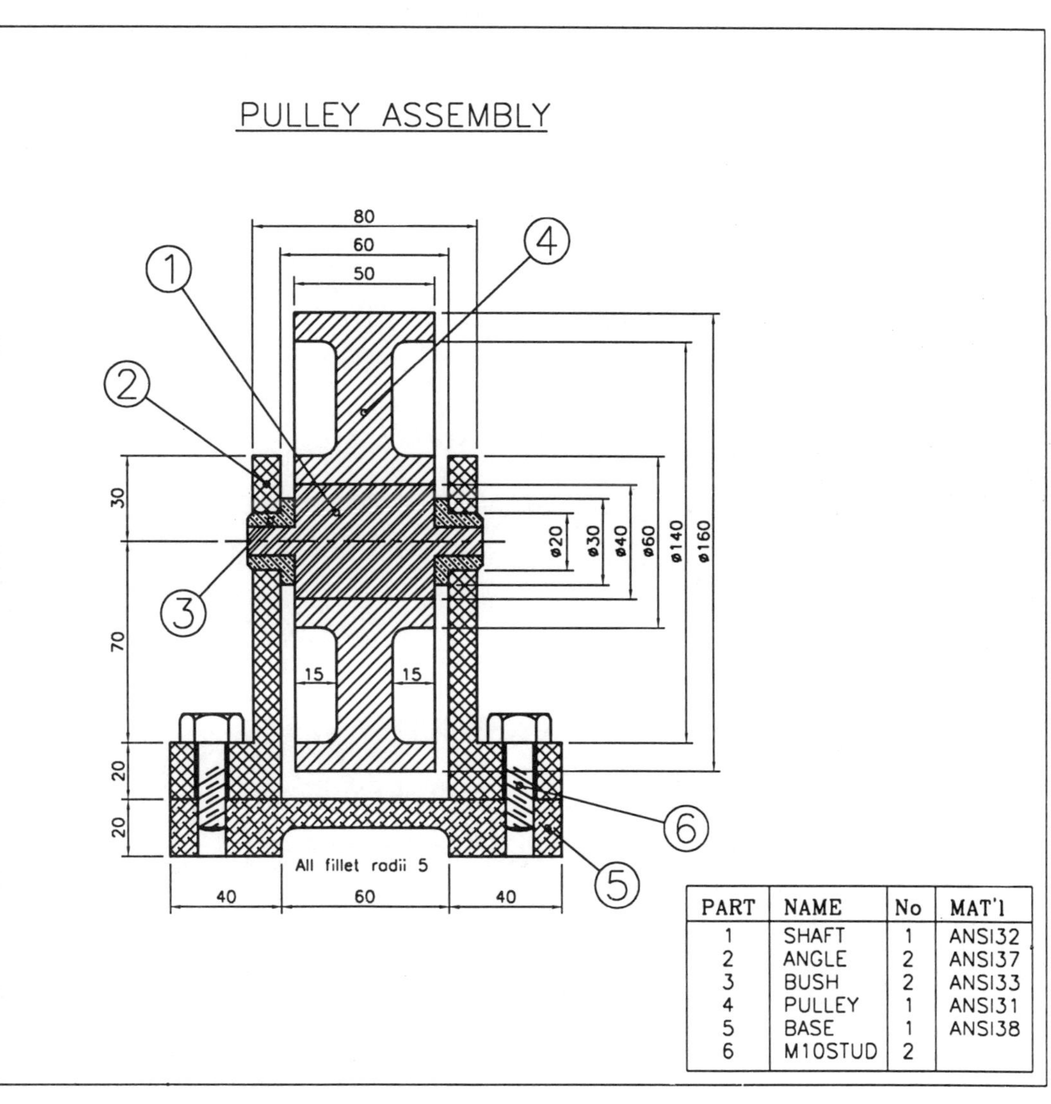

PART	NAME	No	MAT'l
1	SHAFT	1	ANSI32
2	ANGLE	2	ANSI37
3	BUSH	2	ANSI33
4	PULLEY	1	ANSI31
5	BASE	1	ANSI38
6	M10STUD	2	

Assignment 74

Bridge

Using the given sizes, create the bridge arrangement.

Blocks or copy?

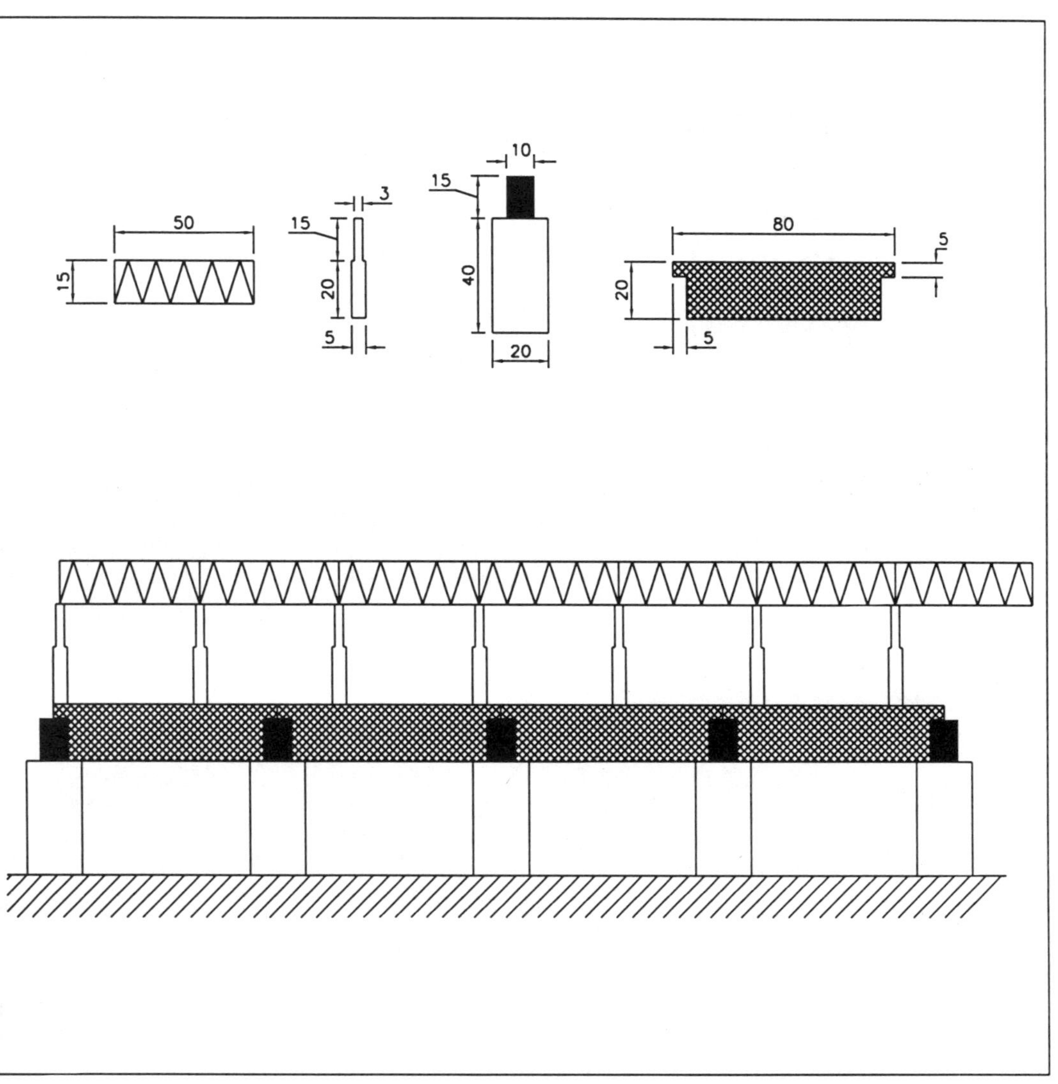
50
15
15
3
20
5
10
15
40
20
80
20
5
5

Assignment 75

Logo 1

Using a grid of 10 and a snap of 5, create a series of logos for an estate agent's business.

Three ideas are given for consideration.

Scale and hatch the final results.

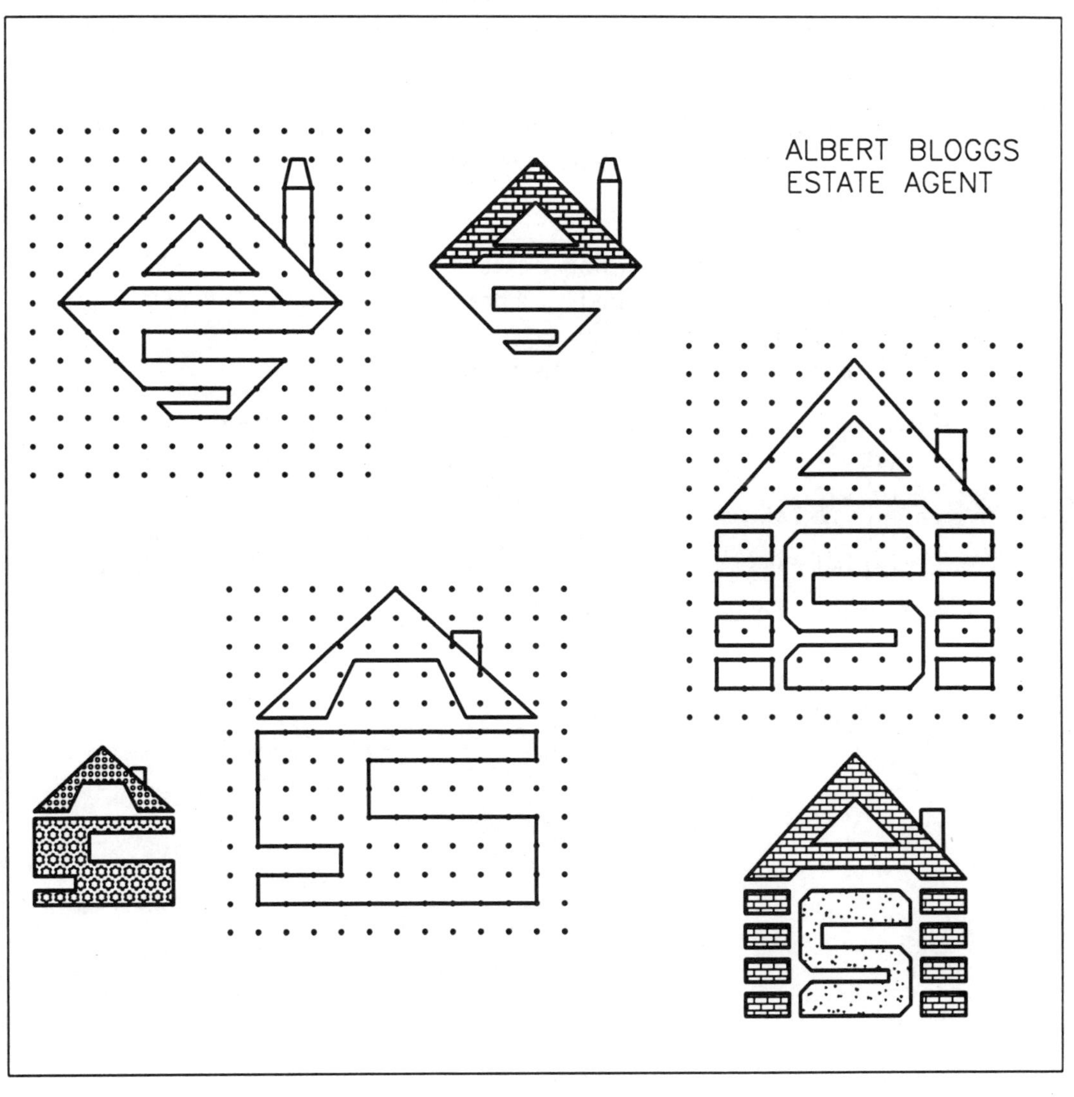
ALBERT BLOGGS
ESTATE AGENT

Assignment 76

3D pyramid

In paper space, set a four viewport configuration and create a 3D faced wire-frame model from the following data:

(a) base 100 square
(b) height 100
(c) 'all-seeing eye' on a sloped face
(d) brick hatching on the four sides
(e) 'stars in the eye' hatching
(f) base hatching – at your discretion.

Alter the viewpoints to display the following 'centred' views:

(a) 3D
(b) top
(c) front
(d) left-side.

Note: watch the hatch scale factor!

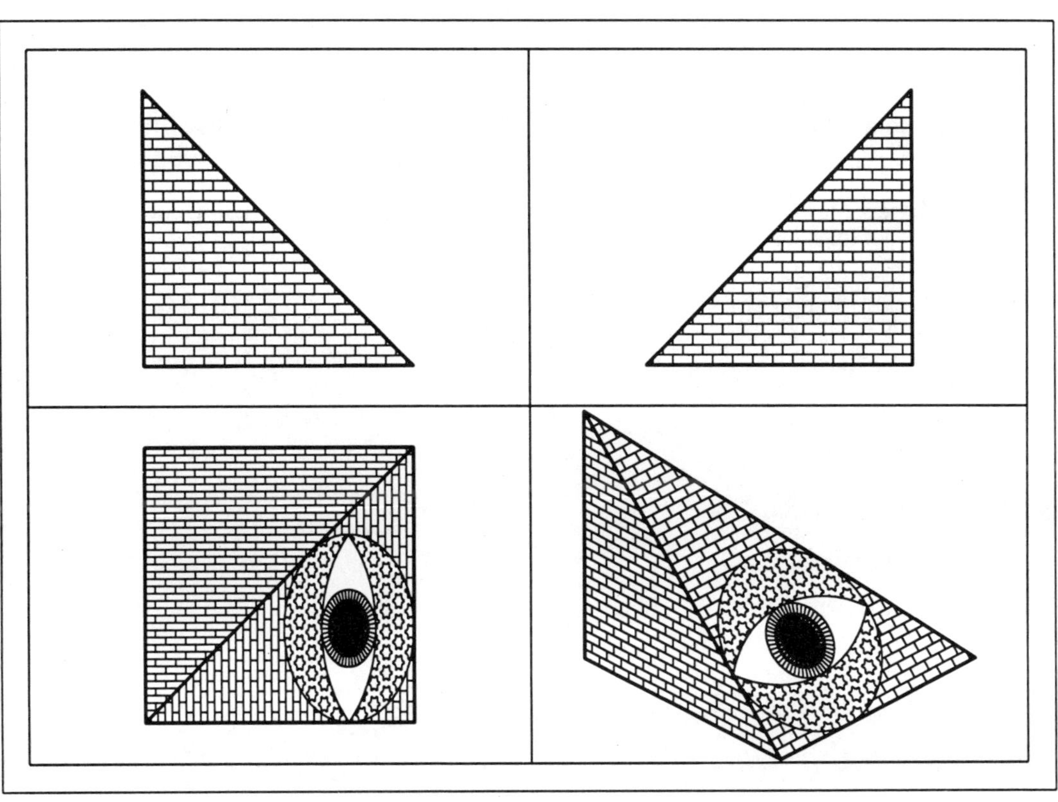

Assignment 77

Logo 2

With a grid of 10 and a snap of 5 create a logo for Boffington University using the given design – or your own?

Make a block of the logo, then insert it at different scales for effect, then:

(a) hatch?
(b) solid?
(c) embellish?

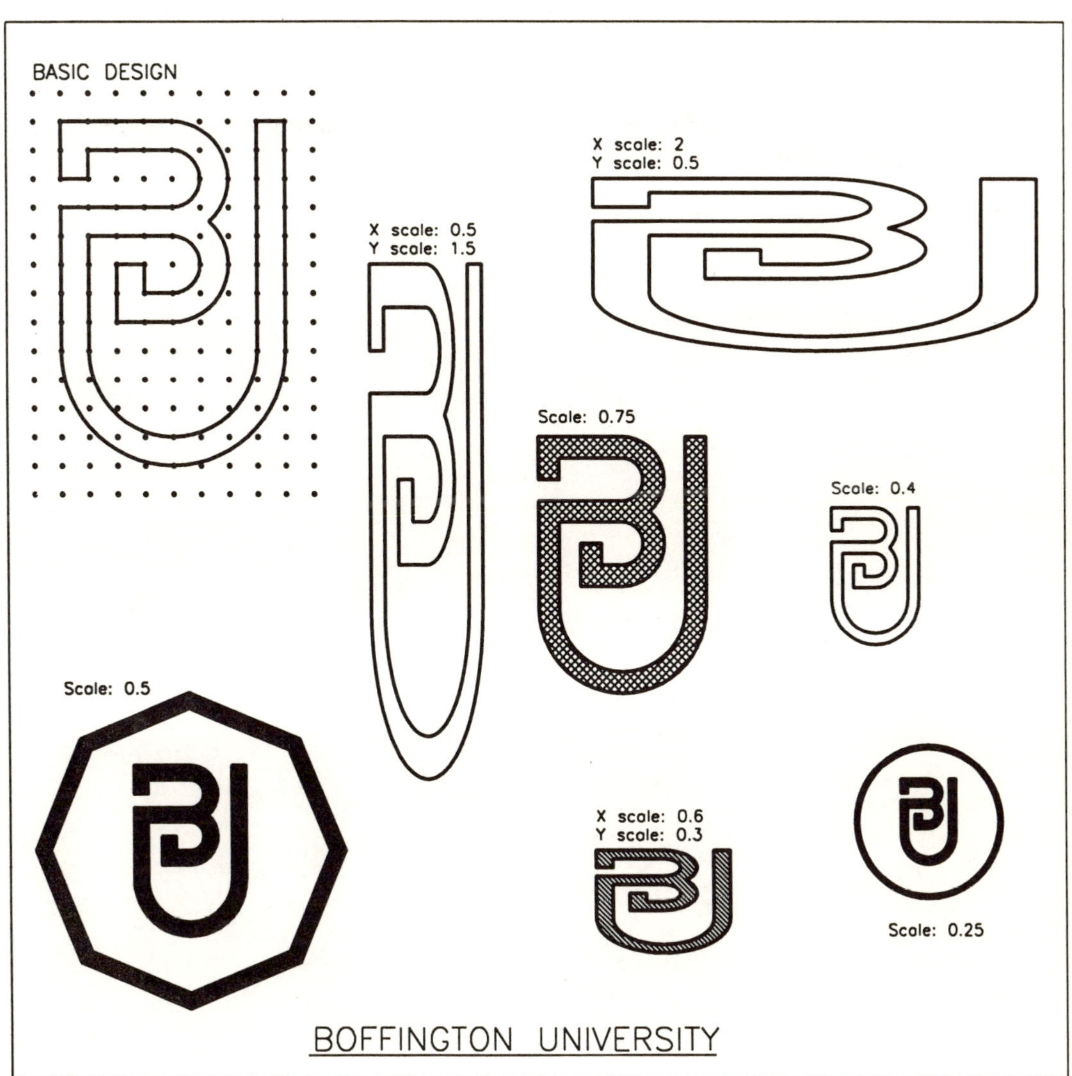
BASIC DESIGN
X scale: 2
Y scale: 0.5
X scale: 0.5
Y scale: 1.5
Scale: 0.75
Scale: 0.4
Scale: 0.5
X scale: 0.6
Y scale: 0.3
Scale: 0.25
BOFFINGTON UNIVERSITY

Assignment 78

Illusions 3

This is the tenth illusion, which I've called perpetual motion and there is no help with it.

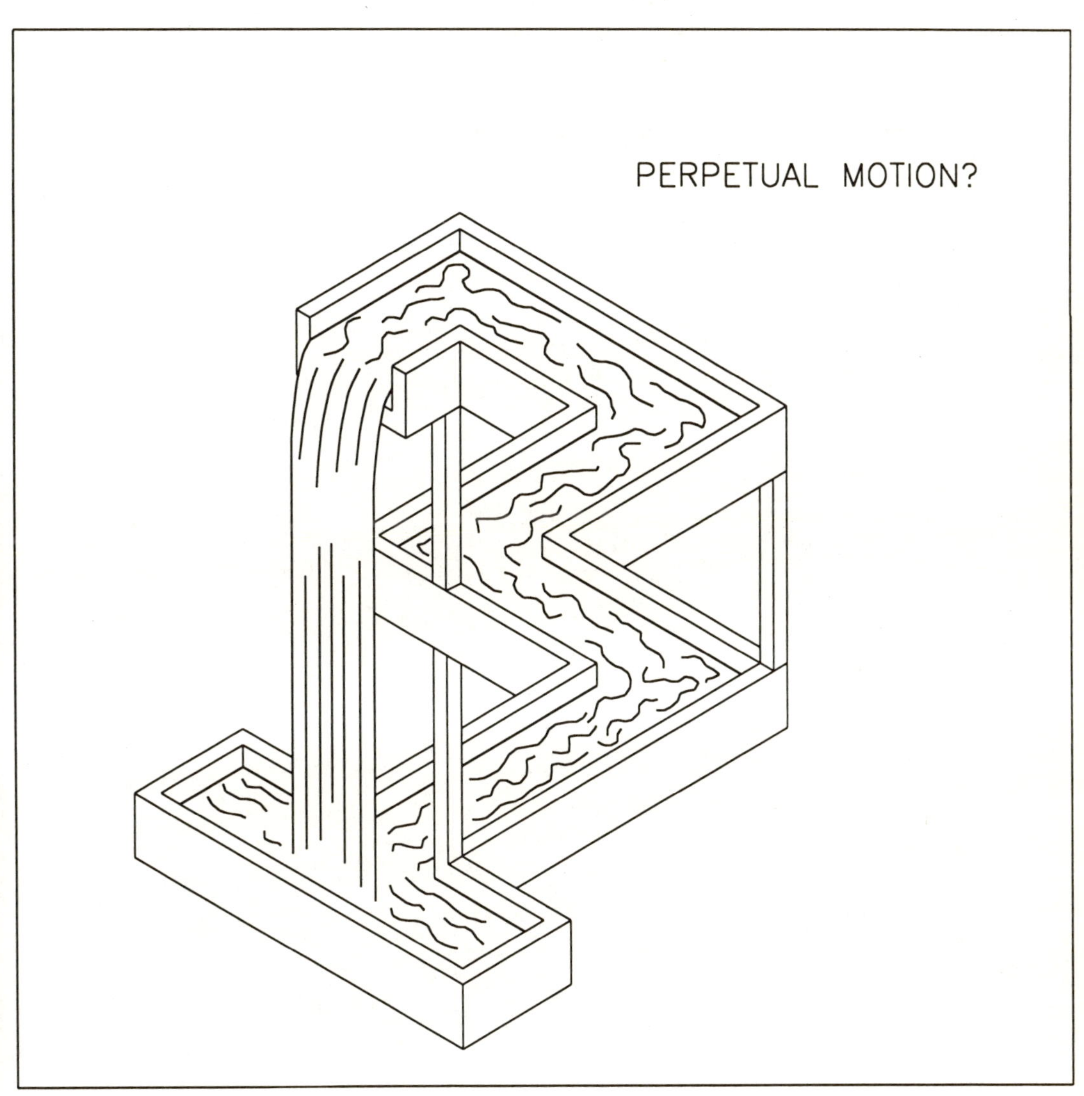
PERPETUAL MOTION?

Assignment 79

An uplifting experience

Draw the nineteenth-century air-mail service.

Bob's
Air
Express

Assignment 80

Take off

No help with this assignment.

Simply draw the view of the fighter.

Getting the size correct can be harder than you would expect.

McDonnell Douglas
F-4C PHANTOM
Jetfighter

Assignment 81

Calling cards

Create a series of calling cards using the basic logo idea.

Note inclusion of the pet symbol from assignment 54, and the fighter from assignment 80.

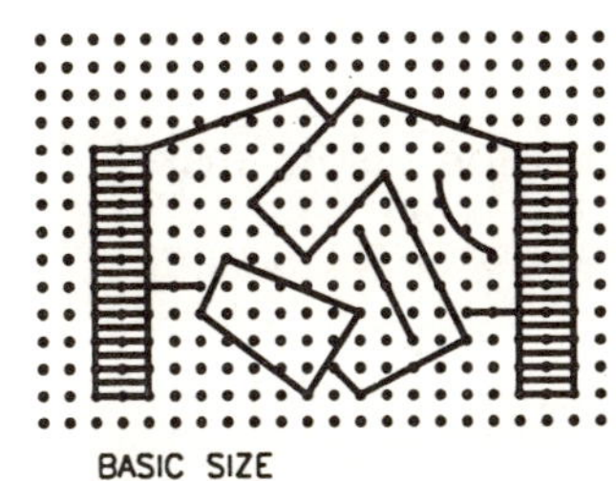
BASIC SIZE

AutoLAND
Pet's
Club

Scale: 0.5

Scale: 0.25

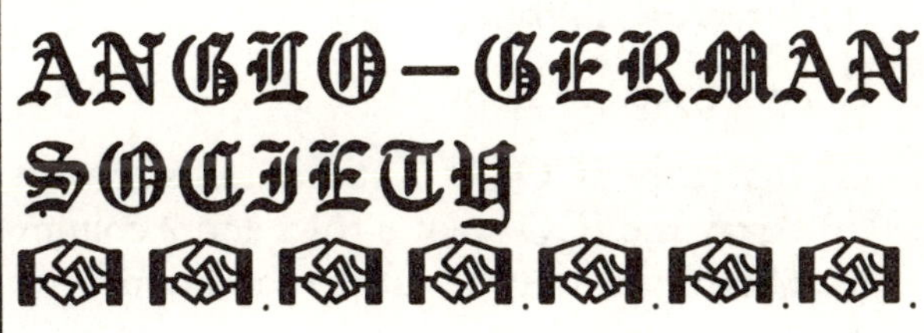
ANGLO-GERMAN
SOCIETY

AutoCAD Flying Club - TOPCAD

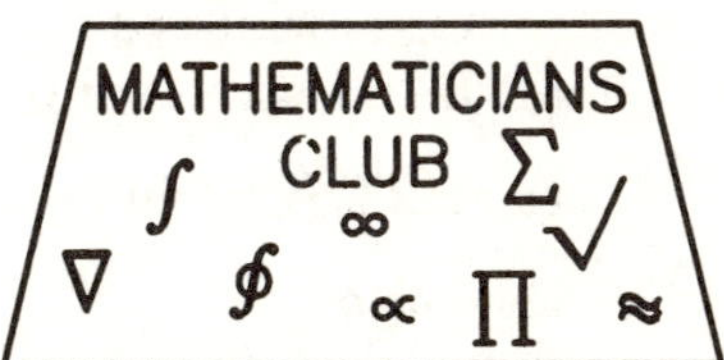
MATHEMATICIANS
CLUB

Assignment 82

Factory floor plan

1. Set to architectural units, then using the information below, make **three WBLOCKS** for the:
   (a) ICOL
   (b) WIND
   (c) TOILET – using your imagination.
2. Use the set-up command with:
   (a) Architectural units
   (b) scale of 3″=1′
   (c) fitted on A3 paper
3. Draw the factory floor.
4. (a) Insert the ICOL at 12 times full size with 90 rotation.
   (b) Array the ICOL For 6 rows and 2 columns.
   (c) Mirror the array about the top boundary.
5. (a) Insert the WIND into one vertical wall with:
   X scale: 60
   Y scale: 8
   Rotation: 90
   (b) Array the WIND for 6 rows, 1 column
   (c) Copy windows to other wall
   (d) Insert WIND into lower wall.
6. Insert TOILET full size
7. Dimension.

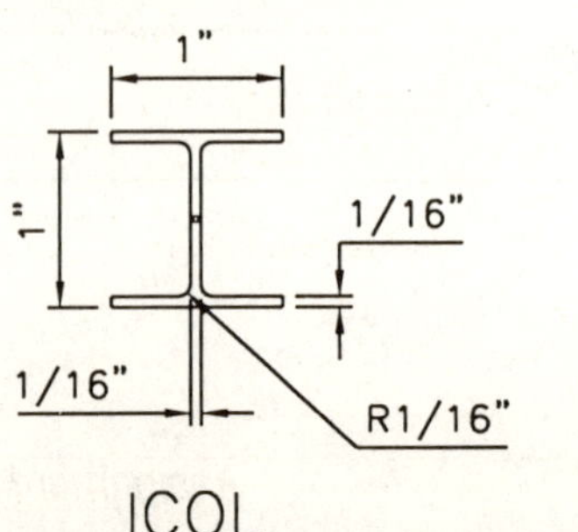

ICOL

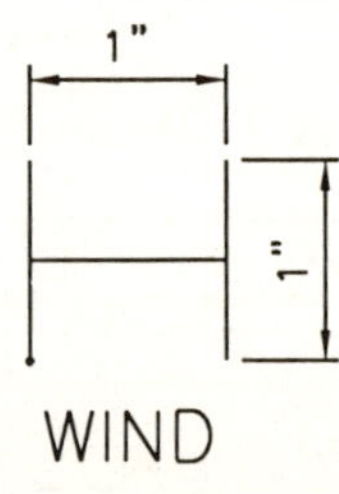

WIND

15'-8"
1' OFFSET
1' OFFSET
10'
10'-2"
CONSTRUCTION LINES
8" OFFSET

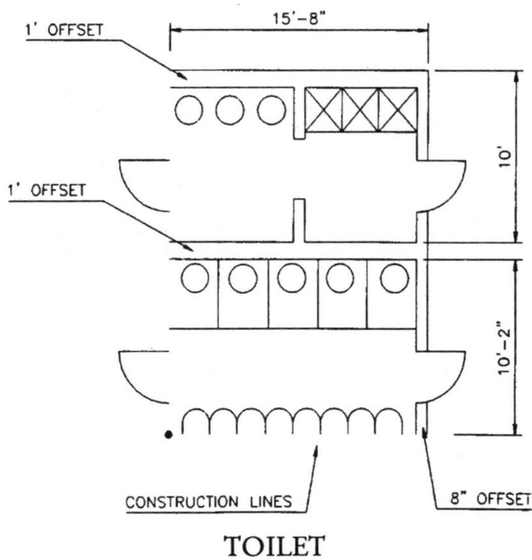

TOILET

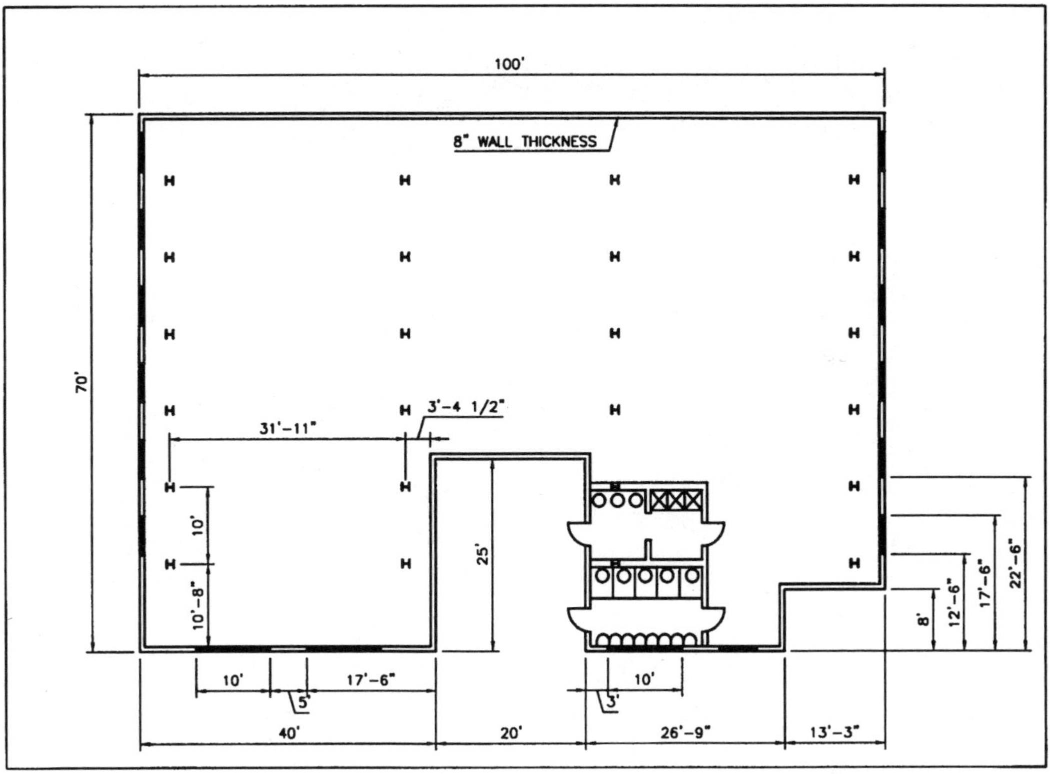

100'
8" WALL THICKNESS
70'
31'-11"
3'-4 1/2"
10'
10'-8"
25'
22'-6"
17'-6"
12'-6"
8'
10'
5'
17'-6"
10'
3'
40'
20'
26'-9"
13'-3"

Assignment 83

Temperature toggle

A very small component, which is to be drawn on A3 paper, so set as follows:

(a) decimal units to 5DP
(b) scale factor of 0.001
(c) grid: 0.01 and snap: 0.005
(d) dimscale?
(e) text height?

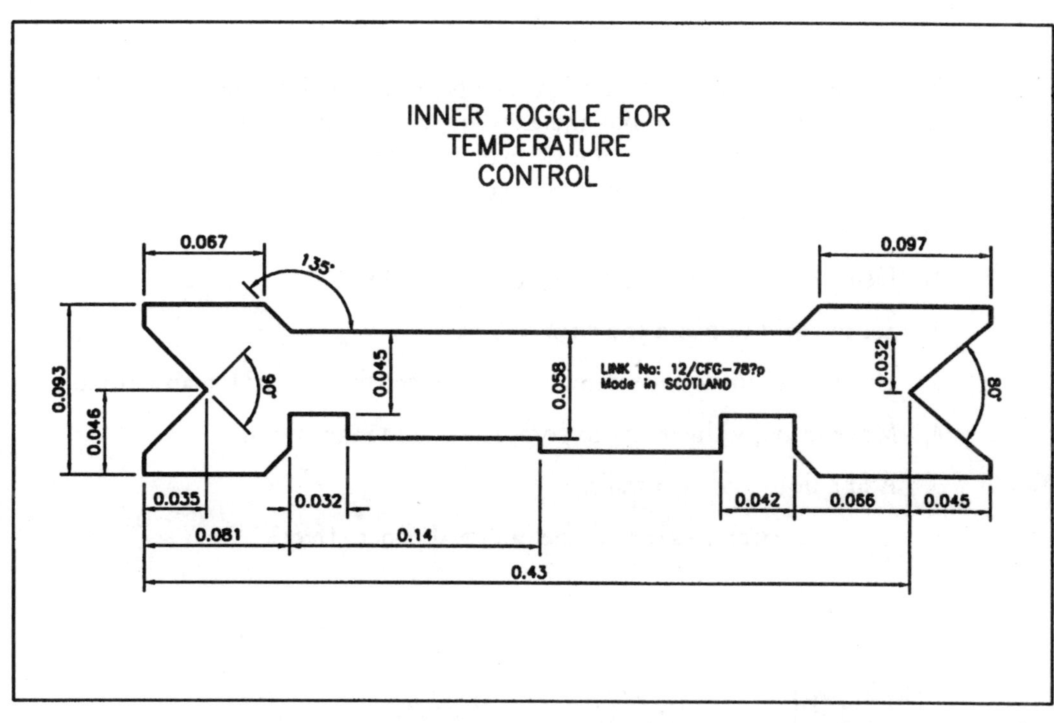
INNER TOGGLE FOR
TEMPERATURE
CONTROL
0.067
135°
0.097
0.093
0.046
90°
0.045
0.058
LINK No: 12/CFG-78?p
Made in SCOTLAND
0.032
80°
0.035
0.032
0.042
0.066
0.045
0.081
0.14
0.43

Assignment 84

Planometric lounge

Many readers will never have heard of a planometric drawing. It is similar to an isometric drawing, but the axes are at 45 degrees and not 30. The drawings produced in planometric may seem 'odd', but the effect is as if you were 'looking down' on an object.
To create the lounge effect:

1. Using drawing aids, set the snap angle to 45.
2. Set the grid to 5 and the snap to 2.5.
3. Create the nine lounge items shown below using the grid/snap setting.
4. Move or copy the items to complete the lounge layout.
5. Add a floor and two walls.
6. Can you hatch to give a carpet and wallpaper effect?

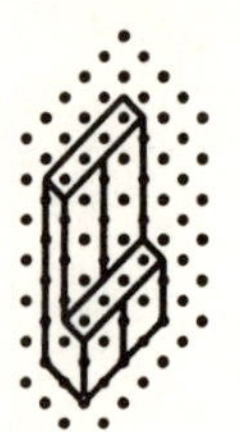

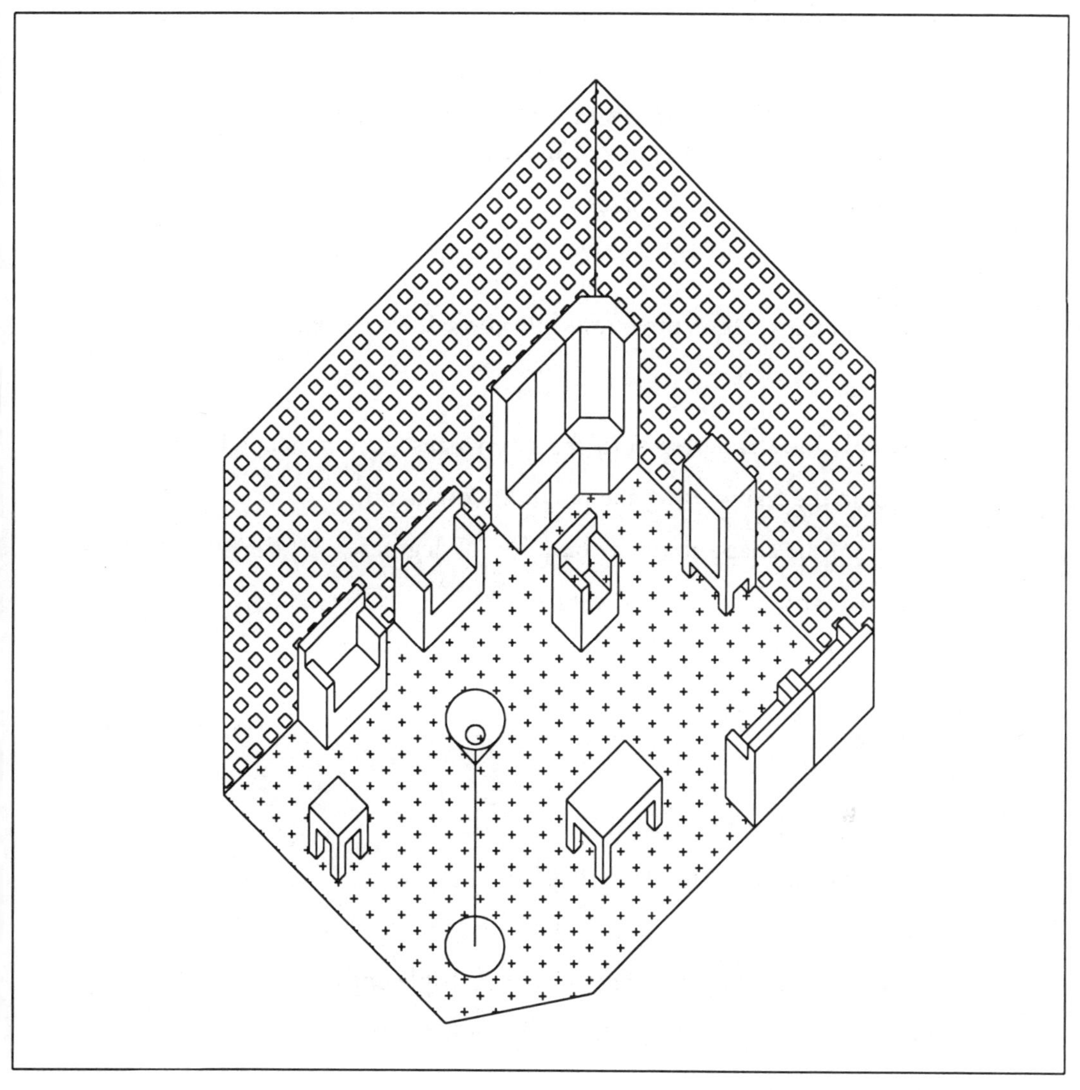

Assignment 85

Bob's tower

This assignment involves several of the modify commands for the three 'designs' which are incorporated in the tower.

Draw the tower using the sizes given.

Design A

1. Line and arc segments – multiple copied or arrayed?

Design B

1. A polyline shape drawn to the given sizes – zoom needed?
2. Spline the shape using the polyedit command.
3. Rotate the shape about its base for 28 degrees.
4. Mirror about the vertical centre.
5. Move the 'top' of the arc.
6. Polar array twice.

Design C

1. Lines for the 'girder' shape.
2. Copy to base of the three 'legs'.
3. Scale the top shape (by 0.5) then array/multiple copy.
4. Stretch the other two shapes then multiple copy.

Finally complete your tower by adding your own refinements.

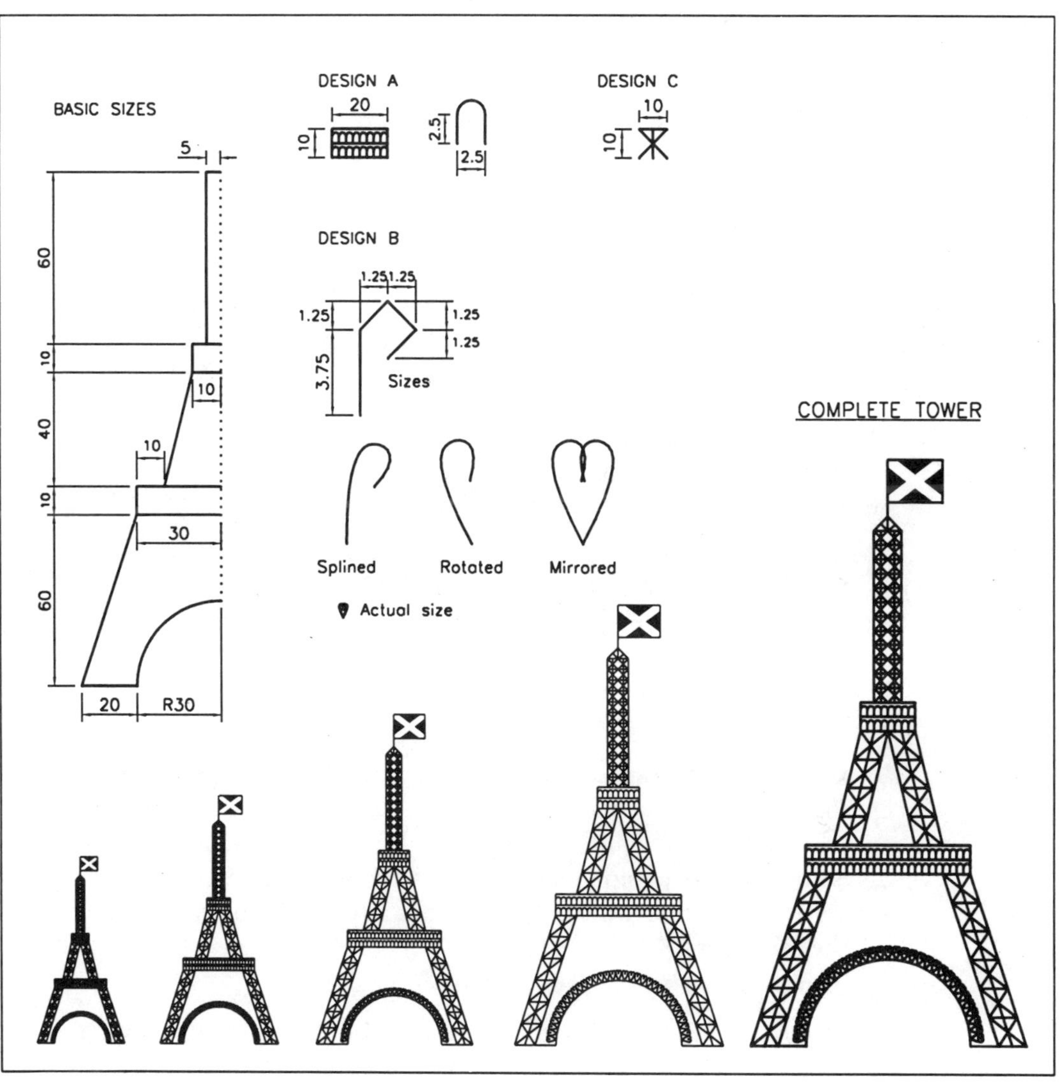
BASIC SIZES
5
60
10
10
40
10
10
30
60
20
R30
DESIGN A
20
10
2.5
2.5
DESIGN C
10
10
DESIGN B
1.25 1.25
1.25
1.25
1.25
3.75
Sizes
Splined
Rotated
Mirrored
Actual size
COMPLETE TOWER

Assignment 86

PCB layout

This is the last assignment and is in four parts:

(a) the board design
(b) the component design
(c) assembling the components on the board
(d) viewing the complete board in 3D.

The assignment uses the elevation/thickness technique as well as the SOLID command (**with FILL off**) to create the various components.

The drawing sheet

1. Set units to decimal and 4DP.
2. Limits 0, 0 to 21, 16 and Zoom-All.
3. Grid 1 and snap 0.25 – or to suit.

(a) *The board*
   1. Set elevation to 0 and thickness to –0.25.
   2. Using a closed polyline, draw the board using the sizes given in Fig. 86(a).
   3. Move the board to one corner of the screen.

(b) *The components*
   1. Using the elevation and thickness values from Fig. 86(b), create the nine components. Remember to have FILL off when using the SOLID command for the 'boxes'.
   2. Some of these components require a bit of thought!
   3. As each component is made, move it to any appropriate part of the screen.

(c) *The assembly*
   Using the MOVE and COPY (and SCALE?) commands, design your own PCB layout using the created components – as many or as little as you want – Fig. 86(c) is a guide only.

(d) *The display*
   View your complete assembly in 3D, the viewpoint being arbitrary. Again, Fig. 86(d) is my display.

(a)

3
2.5
1.75
0.5
0.5
2.5
0.5
1
9
All cut-outs are 0.25 'deep'
4
0.25
.75
0.5
3
15.5

(b)

IC
1.Set ELEV 0, THK 0.375
2.SOLID 1.25x0.5
1.5
1.25
1.Set ELEV 0, THK 1
2.SOLID to sizes
TRANSFORMER
1.25
1.75
1.Set ELEV 0, THK 0.5
2.SOLID boby, 1.75x1.25
3.Set ELEV 0.51, THK 0
4.Draw horiz and vert lines, using a snap of 0.175
SOCKET
GROUND
1.Set ELEV 0, THK 1.5
2.CIRCLE, R0.25
CAPACITOR
1.Set ELEV 0, THK 1
2.CIRCLE, R0.25
0.5
0.25
0.75
2
1.Set ELEV 0, THK 0.75
2.SOLID body
3.Set ELEV 0.76, THK 0
4.Draw, Copy switches
DIP SWITCH
0.5
1.125
1.Set ELEV 0, THK 0.75
2.SOLID body
3.Lines and Ellipse to suit
JUMPS
1.Set ELEV 0, THK 0.5
2.SOLID body
3.Set ELEV 0, THK 0.25
4.Draw 1 pin then ARRAY
(a)13C at 0.0625
(b)2R at 0.4375
ROM CHIP
0.375
0.0625
TWICE FULL
0.75
0.5
0.375
0.5
1.75
1.Set ELEV 0, THK 0.75
2.Draw body with SOLID
3.Set ELEV 0, THK 0.0625
4.Draw tabs
5.Set ELEV 0.0626, THK 0.06
6.Draw polygon
RESISTOR

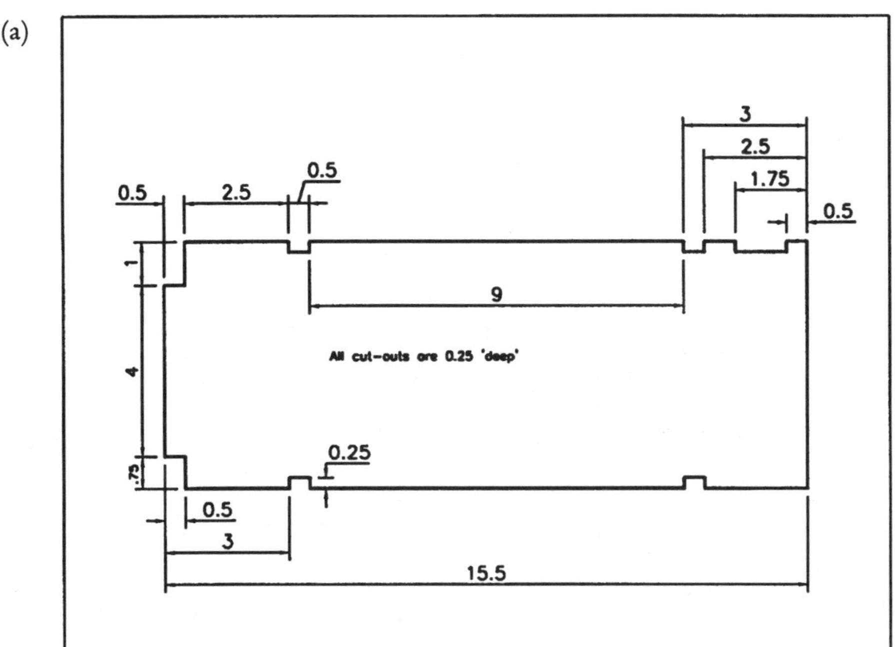

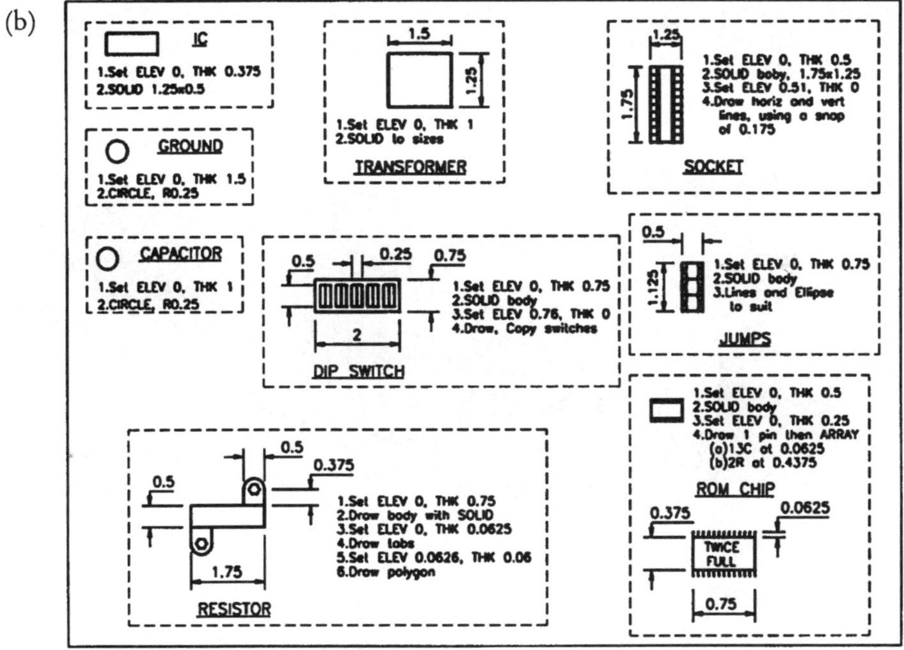

(c)

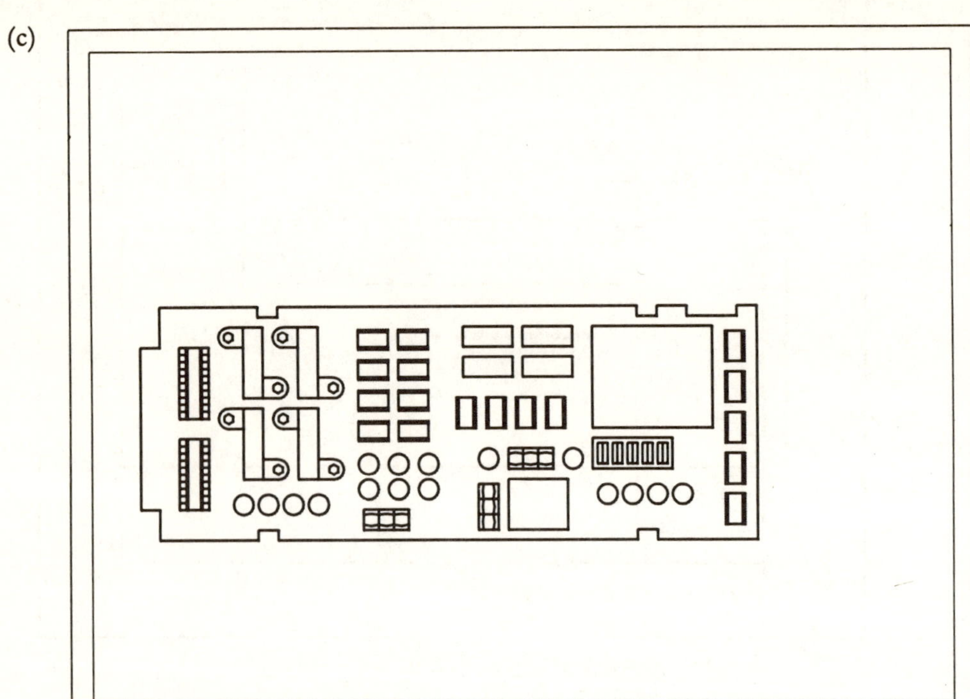

(d)

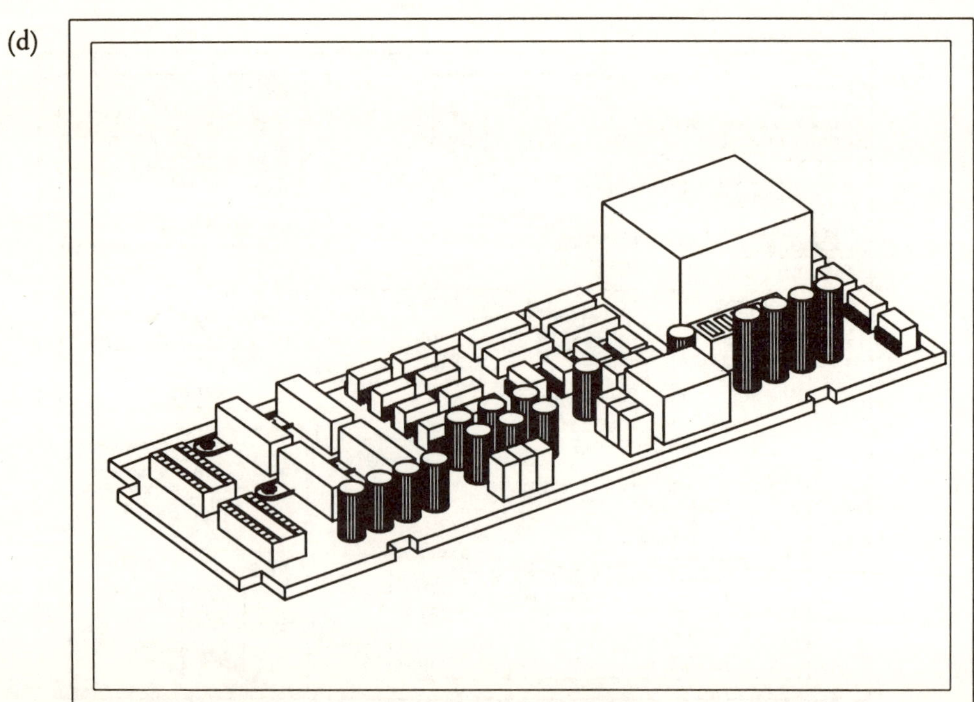